THE BRASS PLAYER'S COOKBOOK

Creative Recipes for a Successful Performance

Published by
Meredith Music Publications
a division of G.W. Music, Inc.
4899 Lerch Creek Ct., Galesville, MD 20765
http://www.meredithmusic.com

Cover and text design by Shawn Girsberger

International Standard Book Number: 1-57463-075-X
Library of Congress Control Number: 2006928398
Printed and bound in U.S.A.

Contents

Foreword

When asked to develop and coordinate the production of *The Brass Player's Cookbook: Creative Recipes for a Successful Performance*, I was very excited about the pedagogical possibilities. Having been a contributing author for the first book in this series, *The Music Director's Cookbook: Creative Recipes for a Successful Program*, I had a fairly good idea of what a similar book—one dedicated to brass players—might offer. Here was an opportunity to create a valuable educational and inspirational resource for anyone involved in making music on a brass instrument. The unique significance of this "cookbook" would not only be a result of its rich and varied content but also of the diversity of its authorship. It was clear to me that this project would require a team of experienced and knowledgeable "master chefs"—individuals who have earned the respect of audiences, students, and colleagues and proven themselves to be exceptional musicians. Thus I began the task of recruiting a "band," filling its seats with individuals who fit the criteria and could provide instructive ideas and concepts.

The subject and target audience for each recipe was left up to the individual writer. The only direction given was that they write something that would help other brass players to improve themselves, their students, or their ensembles. Although the topics covered address a variety of brass-related issues, a number of them focus on the more intellectual and psychological aspects of being a performer—an area too often overlooked in many texts. The fifty-seven authors selected for this project continue to successfully manage the many mental and physical stresses associated with being a brass artist and, as a result, have risen to great heights in their respective areas of expertise. They share their collective wisdom with the utmost sincerity and generosity. Each writer is donating the royalties that they would have earned on this project to the American Music Conference (AMC), a nonprofit affiliate of NAMM, the International Music Products Association. Through their proactive approach, the American Music Conference leads the way in support of music education in America and around the world.

More important than the number of practical and philosophical ideas presented in this publication is the fact that each article is written in the individual writer's own words. This approach allows a reader to more closely experience the personality, style, and spirit of each of these esteemed professionals. If a reader has difficulty finding guidance through the stylized writing of one particular author, they need only turn the page to experience that of another. Perhaps by experiencing these different voices, a reader may increase his or her own ability to relate to a wider range of tutelage.

No matter if you're vegetarian, lactose intolerant, or simply dieting, there's something here for everyone. With an inquisitive mind and an inviting palate, these "recipes" will surely nourish the mind, body, and spirit—providing motivation and inspiration to all.

Buen provecho.

Kenneth Amis
Project Director/Editor

Acknowledgments

To each of the *chefs* who contributed to this publication, I offer my sincere thanks. Each individual responded to our initial invitation with a resounding yes. They were each enthusiastic about being involved in what they felt would be a unique and worthwhile contribution to brass playing and to music education. Their generosity has been exceptional, their expertise unquestionable, and their love of brass playing and music education inspiring. The writings within, presented by them, are based on years of study and experience, and reflect a variety of educational and professional levels.

Profound thanks and admiration are extended to Kenneth Amis, editor and coordinator of this volume. Ken could, and should, write a book on organization and management; his skills are incredible! He is a creative and talented individual to whom I owe a great deal of thanks. Ken tirelessly went about the task of selecting authors, organizing and collecting materials, motivating writers, and editing text with energy and enthusiasm. In addition to being a superb musician, Ken is also an educator of the highest order, which is apparent in the composition of this volume. Thanks to Ken Amis, the world now has a collection of interesting and insightful articles contained in one volume, written by many of today's most outstanding brass players and pedagogues. To Shawn Girsberger, my unending gratitude for her work with Meredith Music Publications and for the artistic layout and cover design of this volume. For leading the way in support of music education in our schools and for their assistance in marketing, thanks to Joe Lamond, President and CEO of NAMM, and Laura Johnson, Associate Executive Director of the American Music Conference. I would also like to offer my sincere appreciation to the many individuals who have encouraged me throughout my career as a writer and publisher.

And finally, to the thousands of music students and their directors who have inspired each of us, our never-ending thanks for your dedication, beautiful music making, and belief that music does make a difference.

Garwood Whaley
President and Founder
Meredith Music Publications

About the Authors

Jeff Adams, trombonist, holds the Jazz Chair in the Army's top touring big band, the Jazz Ambassadors, based in Washington, D.C. He is also a Kanstul Artist. For more information about Jeff including his touring schedule, bio, and MP3 samples of his improvisation, please visit www.SlideAdams.com.

Kenneth Amis, after obtaining a masters degree in composition, became the tuba player of the Empire Brass in 1993. Mr. Amis has served on the faculties of Boston University, Lynn University, and the Pacific Music Festival. He is also the assistant wind ensemble director at Massachusetts Institute of Technology and tuba player of the Palm Beach Opera Orchestra. His many compositions, arrangements, and other offerings for brass players are available from his online store at www.AmisMusicalCircle.com.

Roger Bobo is a world-renowned teacher, virtuoso soloist, and brass legend. He is in demand worldwide as a teacher of all brass instruments, adjudicator at major international competitions, and as a conductor.

Lisa O. Bontrager, horn professor at Penn State University, has performed as a soloist and chamber musician throughout the United States and in Europe and Japan. She performs and has recorded with the Pennsylvania Quintet, the Millennium Brass, and with Michelle Stebleton in the horn duo, MIRRORIMAGE. As a clinician for Holton horns, Bontrager has performed at numerous regional, national, and international workshops of the International Horn Society, also serving on the advisory council of that organization. Her solo CD *Hunter's Moon* was released by Summit Records in 2002.

Velvet Brown, tuba artist, enjoys a professional career as an international soloist and chamber ensemble performer, recording artist, conductor, orchestral player, jazz performer (Howard Johnson's *Gravity!*), and teacher. She has made regular appearances throughout Europe, Japan, Canada, and the United States. She is professor of tuba and euphonium at Pennsylvania State University. Her most noted solo recordings include two CDs, *Velvet* and *Music for Velvet* (Crystal Records), and John Williams' *Tuba Concerto* (Albany Records). Velvet Brown is a Meinl Weston artist.

John Clark, hornist and composer, has performed all over the world with a tremendous diversity of musicians, in a variety of musical arenas: jazz, pop, classical, and commercial studio work. John is professor of horn at the Conservatory of Music, Purchase College, State University of New York. His Web site is www.hmmusic.com.

Dale Clevenger has been principal horn of the Chicago Symphony Orchestra for the past forty years. He is also a soloist, conductor, recording artist, professor of horn at Roosevelt University, father of four, and husband to Alice Render.

Abbie Conant played principal trombone with the Munich Philharmonic for thirteen years before becoming professor of trombone at the Staatliche Hochschule fuer Musik in Trossingen, Germany. Her experiences in the orchestra have become the subject of a 90-minute documentary and was written about in the *Wall Street Journal* and Der Spiegel, and was broadcast on NPR's *Performance Today*. It also makes up the last chapter of Malcolm Gladwell's *New York Times* bestseller, *Blink*. She performs cutting-edge, multimedia, one-woman music theater works in collaboration with her husband, composer William Osborne, and has commissioned many works for trombone.

Jeffrey Curnow is associate principal trumpet of the Philadelphia Orchestra and is on the faculty of the Curtis Institute and Temple University. Formerly principal trumpet of the Dallas Symphony, he has also toured and recorded as a member of the Empire Brass and the New York Trumpet Ensemble.

Master Sergeant Kurt Dupuis is principal trumpet of "The President's Own" United States Marine Band. Prior to joining the band, he was a member of the Atlantic Brass and has performed with the Empire Brass. He taught and was a fellow at Tanglewood and attended the Grand Teton Music Festival.

Peter Ellefson is currently on the trombone faculty of Indiana University and the Alessi Seminar. He is a frequent substitute and extra with the New York Philharmonic and the Chicago Symphony. Prior to his position at Indiana University, he was a member of the Seattle Symphony. Mr. Ellefson's Internet home can be found at www.PeterEllefson.com.

Laurie Frink has been a freelance trumpeter in New York City since the 1970s. She is a member of the faculties of New York University, the New School, and Manhattan School of Music.

Jack Gale played with Buddy Morrow, Maynard Ferguson, Woody Herman, and Buddy Rich, as well as with the small groups of Benny Goodman, Kai Winding, Warren Vaché, and Zoot Sims, among others. He was a featured trombonist and arranger on Garrison Keillor's *American Radio Company* on NPR from 1990 through 1994 and has written extensively for brass quintet.

Wycliffe Gordon enjoys an extraordinary career as a performer, composer, arranger, educator, and conductor, receiving high praise and multiple awards and honors from audiences and critics alike. Gordon tours the world, bringing hard-swinging, straight-ahead jazz to audiences ranging from heads of state to elementary school students. In addition, Gordon is rapidly becoming one of America's most persuasive and committed music educators, and currently serves on the faculty of the jazz studies program at The Juilliard School.

James Gourlay is one of Europe's best-known tuba soloists, teachers, and band conductors. He is has been head of wind and percussion at the Royal Northern College of Music in Manchester, England, and in 2006, became the director of the School of Music at the Royal Scottish Academy of Music and Drama. James Gourlay plays Besson tubas.

Toby Hanks has been the tuba player for the San Antonio Symphony, the Minnesota Orchestra, the Casals Festival Orchestra, the Orchestra Symphonico de Puerto Rico, American Composers Orchestra, New York City Ballet Orchestra, and the New York Brass Quintet. He is currently on the faculty of the Manhattan School of Music, Yale University, Peabody Conservatory, and the University of Maryland.

Dick Hansen, a native of Southern California, graduated from University of Southern California School of Music. He apprenticed with Larry Minick before opening Hansen Brass Restoration in 1984.

Kevin Hayward is the bandmaster of the Salvation Army Canadian Staff Band. He has traveled widely as a clinician, conductor, performer, soloist, and adjudicator. He appears on many albums as a trombonist and has worked with many notable artists and ensembles, including Dudley Bright, Phil Smith, Jens Lindemann, Alain Trudel, the Canadian Brass, the Hannaford Street Silver Band, the International Staff Band, Spiritual to the 'Bone, and Maestro Bramwell Tovey.

Lesley Howie currently teaches tenor horn at the Royal Northern College of Music, Chetham's School of Music in Manchester, and as tenor horn tutor for all of the National Youth Brass band courses (England, Scotland, and Wales). She was the first female player of the famous Black Dyke Band on principal solo horn and now performs with a brass sextet of professional players and regularly appears with the group and as a soloist.

Gregory Hustis, principal horn of the Dallas Symphony Orchestra since 1976, teaches at Southern Methodist University, is artistic director of Music in the Mountains (Durango, Colorado), and is widely known through his numerous solo and chamber music recordings.

Alex Iles, Los Angeles studio trombonist, has toured live as lead/solo trombonist with Maynard Ferguson and Woody Herman. He is currently principal trombonist with the Long Beach Symphony, on the faculty of California State University, Northridge and the California Institute of the Arts, and appears regularly on sessions for motion pictures, records, and television.

Ingrid Jensen, trumpeter, has been highly visible on the jazz scene for over twelve years, making award-winning recordings, performing globally at festivals and clubs, and establishing herself as a first-rate educator at high schools, universities, and jazz camps. She currently has four CDs out as a leader and can be heard on countless others, including Grammy-award-winning Maria Schneider's *Concert in the Garden*. Her current CD, *At Sea*, is available through her Web site www.IngridJensen.com.

Dave Kirk is principal tubist of the Houston Symphony and associate professor at Rice University's Shepherd School of Music. Mr. Kirk enjoys a national reputation for excellence as a performer and pedagogue. He has been a guest performer with many of the great American orchestras, and has given master classes throughout the United States and in Japan.

Craig Knox is principal tuba of the Pittsburgh Symphony Orchestra, founding member of the Center City Brass Quintet, and faculty member at Duquesne and Carnegie Mellon Universities. He was previously principal tuba of the Sacramento Symphony, acting principal tuba of the San Francisco Symphony, and has performed with seven of the major American orchestras. He is a graduate of the Curtis Institute of Music, where he studied with Paul Krzywicki.

Mark H. Lawrence is the principal trombonist with the San Francisco Symphony. He has also been a member of Empire Brass, Summit Brass, and Chicago's Music of the Baroque. He has been on the faculties of Boston University, Northwestern University, and is currently professor of trombone and brass chair at the San Francisco Conservatory of Music. His discography includes many solo, chamber music, and orchestral CDs.

John Marcellus is professor of trombone at the Eastman School of Music and member of the Eastman Brass. He is also music director of the Eastman Trombone Choir and Brighton Symphony Orchestra, and principal trombone of the Chautauqua Symphony Orchestra. He was formerly the principal trombone of the National Symphony Orchestra, assistant principal of Baltimore Symphony, and soloist with the United States Navy Band, Washington, D.C.

Raymond Mase has been trumpeter with the American Brass Quintet since 1973, and is responsible for many of their performance editions of sixteenth-, seventeenth-, and nineteenth-century music. He also serves as chair of the brass department at the Juilliard School and principal trumpet of the New York City Ballet Orchestra. He can be heard on more than 100 recordings and as soloist on the Summit, Deutsche Grammophon, Koch, Troy, Cambria, MHS, and Furious Artisans labels.

Steven Mead has been a professional euphonium soloist for more than twenty years and is professor of euphonium at the Royal Northern College of Music in Manchester, England. He is probably the best-known euphonium player in the world today. Through his teaching, playing, and numerous recordings, he has helped popularize this instrument and inspire the next generation. Steven is a clinician and artist consultant for Besson. His Web site is www.euphonium.net.

Brad Michel, recording engineer and session producer for Harmonia Mundi USA, Burbank, Calif. and owner of Clarion Productions Boston, has recorded hundreds of critically acclaimed and award-winning CDs. Brad trained as a trumpet player with David Greenhoe, Vincent Cichowicz, and Charles Geyer.

Gregory Miller is currently chairman of the wind and percussion division and associate professor of horn at the University of Maryland School of Music, College Park. Formerly a member of the internationally renowned Empire Brass, Mr. Miller maintains an active solo and recital career and is a member of the Palm Beach Opera Orchestra.

Bob Montgomery is an internationally recognized jazz artist who has appeared throughout the world with many of the jazz greats as well as with his own quartets and quintets. As an educator, Bob has been awarded "Teacher of the Year," "Jazz Educator and Performer of the Year," "Colorado Jazz Educator of the Year," and "Alumni of Merit Award for Distinguished Service in the Arts." He has served both Kansas and Colorado as State International Association for Jazz Education president, and has directed all-state jazz ensembles in several states.

Jennifer Montone is the principal horn of the Philadelphia Orchestra. Formerly principal horn of the St. Louis Symphony, she has also held positions with the Dallas symphony and New Jersey Symphony Orchestras. She is on the faculty of the Aspen Music Festival and School, and has performed with the Santa Fe Chamber Music Festival, La Jolla Summerfest, Marlboro Music Festival, and the Chamber Music Society of Lincoln Center. An aspiring soloist, as well, she is the thankful recipient of numerous awards and grants.

Daniel Perantoni is tuba professor of music at Indiana University. "M.P.," as his students call him, is a legendary tuba artist, teacher, and pedagogue, as well as a trailblazer in a variety of genres. He is a founding member of the Summit Brass, Symphonia, and the St. Louis Brass Quintet, and has released numerous solo albums and chamber music CDs.

Marc Reese joined the Empire Brass Quintet in 1996 and performs internationally as chamber musician, soloist, and master clinician. He has performed with the New York Philharmonic, Cleveland Orchestra, and Boston Symphony, and has appeared at Marlboro, Tanglewood, and the Pacific Music Festival. He currently resides in South Florida, where he serves as head of the brass department at Lynn University's Conservatory of Music. For more information, visit www.MarcReese.com.

Ronald Romm, trumpeter extraordinaire, is a founding and former member of the world-famous Canadian Brass. A Yamaha performing artist and clinician, Mr. Romm is professor of trumpet at the University of Illinois at Urbana-Champaign, and continues a successful international performing and recording career as a soloist and member of the Ronald and Avis Romm Trumpet and Piano Duo.

Mike Roylance has been the tuba player with the Boston Symphony Orchestra and the Boston Pops since 2003. Mike received his master's degree at DePaul University and was a member of the Civic Orchestra of Chicago. Prior to Chicago, Mike spent twelve years gaining vast experience in Orlando, Fla., playing all styles of music. Mike teaches at the New England Conservatory and Boston University.

Jon Sass is a native New Yorker who is surely the most innovative tubist of our time. His unique style, sound, and versatility can be heard on more than seventy CDs. He has traveled the world for more than twenty-five years playing with high-profile groups in several music genres.

Ralph Sauer joined the Los Angeles Philharmonic in 1974 after six years as principal trombone with the Toronto Symphony. His teachers were Robert Harper (Philadelphia Orchestra) and Emory Remington (Eastman School of Music).

Susan Slaughter has been principal trumpet of the St. Louis Symphony since 1973. She is recognized as being the first woman principal trumpet in a major symphony orchestra. She is a featured soloist with orchestras in the St. Louis area and on the West Coast. In addition to having served on the board of the International Trumpet Guild, Ms. Slaughter founded the International Women's Brass Conference and the Monarch Brass Ensemble.

Phyllis Stork was born in New York City and attended the High School of Performing Arts and the Juilliard School. Performance credits include: Lincoln Center's "Young Artists Program," the New York Trumpet Ensemble under Gerard Schwarz, the Alexander Schneider Festival Orchestra, and the Marlboro Festival Orchestra. She has also performed with Wynton Marsalis, Yo-Yo Ma, and Rudolph Serkin. Phyllis, along with her husband John, owns and operates Stork Custom Mouthpieces, creating mouthpieces for all brass musical instruments. Stork Custom Mouthpieces are distributed worldwide.

Deanna Swoboda is assistant professor of music at Western Michigan University, where she teaches tuba and euphonium, and performs with the Western Brass Quintet, a resident faculty ensemble. Swoboda holds degrees from the University of Idaho and Northwestern University, and is completing studies for the doctor of musical arts degree from Arizona State University.

David Taylor, bass trombonist, lives, performs, and teaches in New York. He has recorded many solo and chamber music CDs, and maintains a strong international performance career. He has won the National Academy of Recording Arts and Sciences' Most Valuable Player, and Virtuoso Awards five times (the most it could be awarded). His Web site is: www.DaveTaylor.net.

Kenneth Thompkins was appointed principal trombone of the Detroit Symphony Orchestra in 1997 by Neeme Jarvi. He also performs with Detroit Chamber Winds and is on the faculty of Wayne State University.

Demondrae Thurman is assistant professor of tuba/euphonium at the University of Alabama. Demondrae is extremely active as a soloist and clinician, having performed all over North America and Europe. Demondrae is a member of the Sotto Voce Quartet and the Brass Band of Battle Creek. He can be heard on several recordings on the Summit Records label, including his debut solo recording entitled *Soliloquies*.

Richard Todd leads a varied career as a concert artist, jazz musician, recording artist, orchestral player, and educator. With six solo CDs to date, as well as more than a dozen chamber, jazz, and orchestral recordings, more than one thousand film scores, solo appearances at both Carnegie Hall and the Hollywood Bowl, and regular appearances at many of America's finest chamber music festivals, Richard Todd is in constant demand as a performer. He is principal horn of the Los Angeles Chamber Orchestra and on the faculty of the Henry Mancini Institute.

Adam Unsworth is a member of the horn section of the Philadelphia Orchestra. He is also instructor of horn and coordinator of brass repertoire at Temple University's Boyer College of Music. Mr. Unsworth's Internet address is www.AdamUnsworth.com.

Warren Vaché has been a professional cornetist, jazz soloist, and recording artist for over thirty years, and is still working on all these recipes. For more information, go to www.WarrenVache.com or do the right thing and buy one of his CDs. Even old cornet players have to eat and pay the rent.

Tom Varner is a jazz French hornist and composer. He has eleven CDs out as a leader, and he plays on more than seventy others. Please visit www.TomVarnerMusic.com.

William VerMeulen enjoys equal success as soloist, pedagogue, orchestral principal horn, and chamber musician. He is professor of horn at the Shepherd School of Music at Rice University and principal horn with the Houston Symphony. Professor VerMeulen enjoys a reputation as a world-class horn soloist and teacher whose students routinely win jobs.

Charles Vernon has been bass trombonist with the Baltimore Symphony Orchestra, the San Francisco Symphony Orchestra, the Philadelphia Orchestra, and currently the Chicago Symphony Orchestra. He has made many recordings and has been a part of several commissioning projects, including a concerto for alto, tenor, bass trombones, and orchestra by Christian Lindberg.

John Wallace, Scottish trumpet player turned educationalist, is now the principal of the Royal Scottish Academy of Music and Drama. His playing career spanned three decades out of London with the Royal Philharmonic, London Symphony, and Philharmonia Orchestras. Composers from Malcolm Arnold to James Macmillan and Sir Peter Maxwell Davies have written concertos for him.

Frøydis Ree Wekre, a native of Oslo, Norway, is a professor of horn and chamber music at Norwegian Academy of Music. Formerly co-principal horn with the Oslo Philharmonic Orchestra for twenty-five years, she has been active worldwide as a soloist, recording artist, master class holder, lecturer, and jury member. She is an honorary member of the International Horn Society, and her book *Thoughts on Playing the Horn Well* has been translated into several languages.

David Werden was solo euphoniumist with the U.S. Coast Guard Band for over twenty years and is currently instructor of euphonium and tuba at the University of Minnesota. He has published forty arrangements for brass, as well as four books, and developed www.DWerden.com (www.TubaEuph.com).

Jeremy West is a cornetto player and founding member of the renowned and pioneering ensemble His Majestys Sagbutts & Cornetts. He is director of Christopher Monk Instruments (manufacture of cornetti and serpents), which distributes instruments worldwide to both amateur and professional players. He teaches at the Royal College of Music in London and can be found at www.jeremywest.co.uk.

Gail Williams joined the Chicago Symphony Orchestra in December 1978, and was appointed associate principal horn in 1984, a position she held until her retirement from the orchestra in 1998. She has been a member of the Chicago Lyric Opera Orchestra, and is currently principal horn of the Grand Teton Music Festival Orchestra. As featured horn soloist, Ms. Williams has performed with the Chicago Symphony Orchestra, San Antonio Symphony, Sinfonia da Camera, Syracuse Symphony, and a number of regional orchestras. She is a horn professor at Northwestern University and a Charles Deering McCormick Professor of Teaching Excellence.

R. Douglas Wright has been the principal trombonist of the Minnesota Orchestra since 1995. He is a former member of the Empire Brass Quintet and has previously held the principal trombone position of the Cleveland Orchestra. Mr. Wright has performed as featured soloist with a number of orchestras, including numerous times with the Minnesota Orchestra, and has performed recitals and taught master classes around the world.

Douglas Yeo is bass trombonist of the Boston Symphony, music director of the New England Brass Band, and on the faculty of Boston's New England Conservatory of Music. In addition to bass trombone, he frequently plays serpent, ophicleide, buccin, and contrabass trombone in modern and period instrument ensembles. His award-winning Web site is www. yeodoug.com.

Maximizing Your Practicing Time on Three Quick Improv Lessons

Jeff Adams

INGREDIENTS:
Pencil
Manuscript paper
Metronome
Your horn
Fake book
Aebersold Volumes 1 and 54 (optional)

SERVES:
All instrumentalists.

Lesson 1

Here is a sample of the formula I use with my improv students.

We are now faced with the task of improvising over the changes to a standard tune. Find one in the Aebersold books without any min7(♭5) or 7(♭9) chords in it. "Satin Doll" is an excellent choice. Where do we begin?

1. To analyze the chord changes, you must have a basic understanding of the diatonic 7 chords built on each of the degrees of the major scale. For example, let's take C major. The scale is C D E F G A B. You will need to write this on manuscript paper. Take each degree of the scale and stack thirds above it, lines above lines, spaces above spaces, until you have four notes. You should then have: C–E–G–B; D–F–A–C; E–G–B–D; F–A–C–E; G–B–D–F; A–C–E–G; B–D–F–A. You will notice that each of these notes is in the correct key of C, with no sharps/no flats. If we were working in E major, you would need to write in the correct accidentals in front of each note. The properties of the written chords are Cmaj7, Dmin7, Emin7, Fmaj7, G7, Amin7, Bmin7(♭5). These respective properties are the same, no matter what major scale you use; you just change the letter name in front appropriately. Some of you have probably recognized the ii–V–I pattern in there already: Dmin7–G7–Cmaj7.

2. Analyze the chord changes so you know what keyality you are in. (I say "keyality," because I don't want you to think "major scale;" I want you to think key signature.) When you see a ii-V–I pattern, you should indicate to yourself the keyality or key signature. You don't want to concentrate on the C major scale; you want to play in that key ("no sharps/no flats") but based on the root of the chord you are on at that moment and reflective of the guide tones. (See next step.)

3. Go through the chords for the tune once again and write in the 3rd and 7th. These are called guide tones, the meat of the chord. They are what make you sound like you know what you are doing when improvising, if you utilize them properly (leading from one chord to the next with them).
4. Once you know the keyality of each and every chord and have written in the guide tones, you are ready to practice.
5. Set the metronome at quarter note = 92 or so. You will now play five choruses (marked A–E below) on the tune at this slow tempo, which gives you plenty of time to think while you are playing.
6. Chorus A: melody. Chorus B: roots. Chorus C: half notes. Utilize guide tones; try to hear themes. Chorus D: quarter notes. Utilize guide tones; try to hear themes. Chorus E: Improvise freely.
7. Be careful to play in perfect time and with a great sound at all times!

Lesson 2

Here is the next scale we need to know backward and forward so we can feel even more comfortable with improvisation: **harmonic minor**. Let's use the harmonic minor scale starting on A. It is A B C D E F G♯.

Remember to grab your manuscript paper and stack your chords.

Chord 1	A–C–E–G♯	=	Amin(maj7)
Chord 2	B–D–F–A	=	Bmin7(♭5)
Chord 3	C–E–G♯–B	=	Cmaj7(♯5)
Chord 4	D–F–A–C	=	Dmin7
Chord 5 with the 9 added	E–G♯–B–D–F	=	E7(♭9)
Chord 6	F–A–C–E	=	Fmaj7
Chord 7	G♯–B–D–F	=	G♯ diminished

Isn't that interesting! Just like the major scale chord properties, no matter what harmonic minor scale you write, the same chord-property rule applies; the only variable is the note name in front of the chord property. Hopefully, you see some new possibilities for your chord analysis and, most importantly, you see the IImin7(♭5)–V7(♭9)–Imin(maj7). Whenever you see this kind of combination, I'm sure you now know what mode you'll use. Keyalities get a little tricky with the harmonic minor, but they still work. For instance, the keyality for A harmonic is G♯. For G harmonic, it is B♭, E♭, and F♯. See what I mean?

Lesson 3

Now it is time for the diatonic 7 chords for the melodic minor (ascending version).

Using the ascending melodic minor scale starting on C, our keyality has only one flat: E♭. Chords then are:

C–E♭–G–B = Cmin(maj7)

D–F–A–C = Dmin7

E♭–G–B–D = E♭maj7(♯5)

F–A–C–E♭	=	F7
G–B–D–F	=	G7
A–C–E♭–G	=	Amin7(♭5)
B–D–F–A	=	Bmin7(♭5)

This scale is most frequently used over the first and third degree of the scale situations, and most importantly, over altered chords. The C melodic minor scale would be utilized over a B7alt. Any time you have a dominant 7 chord that has been highly altered, you just go up a half step from the root and play in the keyality of the melodic minor, starting on that note a half step up from the root: G7alt = A♭ melodic minor, C7alt = D♭ melodic minor, etc. Hope this gives all of you some more ideas and creative options!

Maximized Practice Time

Now that you have some new information pertaining to improvisation, how can you best utilize it during your practice time? There are a couple of quick tips I can give you.

The first is to break up your practice time into a number of 10- to 15-minute sessions. It has been proven that the brain can focus better during these short sessions to retain all you have accomplished, as opposed to the standard nonstop hour or two or three that most spend. This way, every time you come back after a break, your brain is fresh, maximizing the retention of your efforts and accomplishments.

The second is targeted practice. Decide what you want to accomplish in your short session and only work on that. Never practice what you can already do. Work on something you find challenging or difficult. Try a new technique or an improvisation concept.

Finally, in your improvisation practice, try to incorporate the elements of good composition to create continued interest for your listeners, and remember that variety is the spice that keeps your listener focused on your solo. Of course, a little space between phrases is also good so they can process your statements.

Good luck! ➤●

Are You Just Another Crescendoing Vibrator?

Kenneth Amis

When brass students are told to sing with their instrument or to bring out the music, they often simply play louder and with more vibrato. What performance ingredients do you consciously mix in order to be musically expressive and add a personalized flavor to your performances?

Most of us begin phrasing by carefully applying the composer's markings. However, following all the markings on the page is being responsible, not necessarily imaginative or musical. Every nuance and gesture that contributes to a brilliant performance cannot and, for the sake of spontaneity, variety, and logistics, *should not* be included on a score. Composers write "notes," which, as the word implies, only offer an outline of what a performer is required to do. In order to experience the full potential and variety within the music, a performer must supplement the markings on the page with his or her own interpretive gestures, which should not only support the composer's notes, but also show imagination and flexibility.

INGREDIENTS:
A sensitivity to the expressive potential of each phrase
Imagination
A commitment to using more than just volume and vibrato to be expressive

SERVES:
All performers.

Assuming a basic level of instrumental proficiency, we have at our disposal five basic ingredients: volume, articulation, rhythm, pitch, and sound color. Yet, how many of us seek to use these tools in a balanced and conscientious way?

Volume
Brass players are particularly apt to overuse and abuse this ingredient. Even when soloing, brass students attempting to be more expressive will reach for volume as an ingredient before considering any other. This knee-jerk reaction to phrasing often makes brass performances sound one-dimensional and unsuitable for baroque and classical period music. Although it may be possible, with enough ingenuity, to prepare a varied, nutritional, and tasty meal using only baking powder and onions, a much better dining experience will surely result from a more imaginative and balanced use of ingredients. Because changes in volume are relatively easy for the average listener to hear, if overused, they can quickly become the least captivating of performance techniques.

Articulation

Exclusive use of "ta" through a rhythmic piece or "da" through a lyrical one can eventually lead to monotony. String players use a myriad of bow strokes that are not marked by the composer to create an affect, and, if we are attempting to sing through our instruments, we should not forget that vocalists spend years developing their diction and using the distinction between consonant and vowel sounds in a given text to further articulate expressive points in the music. A brass soloist should not try to articulate every note differently but should certainly avoid articulating all notes identically, especially when playing a vocal transcription—a piece whose affect is, in part, dependent on such variety. (Composers are very aware of how the beginning of a word relates to the affect of the music.) Bringing attention to a special note or series of notes in a phrase by slightly changing its/their articulation shows an added flexibility to your phrasing and alleviates the necessity to crescendo into all of your "special moments."

Rhythm

Without changing the tempo of a passage, a performer can draw attention to key moments in the music through minute shifts of its rhythms against its pulse. This can serve to draw a listener's attention to a change in the momentum of the music (e.g., playing one or several notes on the "front or back side" of the beat), a change in its timbre (e.g., slightly shortening notes in brighter textures), or even its harmonic tension (e.g., holding an exceptionally dissonant note a few milliseconds longer before resolving it). Whether one is doing dramatic *rubato* in romantic music or acute momentary manipulations in less elastic music, rhythm is a difficult ingredient to master. Its use requires a strong sense of the pulse or flow of the music. (Sometimes tempo fluctuation is appropriate if it is consistent with the flow of the music.) When administered with precision, rhythm endows a performer's phrasing with character more clearly than any other performance ingredient. Great performers from Glenn Gould to Wynton Marsalis have all mastered the discreet use of rhythm to reveal key points within phrases. The use of this ingredient should be conscientiously considered when developing one's interpretation of a musical line.

Pitch

The technique of inflecting the pitch of a note higher or lower to give added direction or character should be discreet. It is important that one always stays within the boundaries of what would be considered "in tune." It is quite common, for example, for a cellist playing a slow movement of a Bach cello suite to slightly bend a dissonant pitch toward its resolution at a cadence (e.g., leading to tonic). This increases the inherent harmonic tension of the moment, giving the line more direction. The key is to hear and understand when "just" intonation versus "tempered" intonation is being violated so that our playing never breaks the "in tune" boundary. If your just and tempered intonation is good, it is simply a matter of learning how far away from those tunings you can inflect a note before good tension turns bad for any given register and tempo. Another important factor to consider is *when* during the playing of a note its pitch should be inflected—at the very beginning, in the middle, or towards its end? Once these choices are understood, actually doing it on a brass instrument is not difficult yet shows a mature diversity in one's phrasing.

Sound Color

Whether you call it "timbre," "color," or "sound quality," it's arguably the most important component of your expressive voice. Unfortunately, many brass players tend to base decisions on what timbre to use on only two criteria—who the composer is and whether the music is lyrical or not. Using vibrato is certainly a means of *enlivening* one's sound. Unfortunately, many performers are under the misguided belief that vibrato alone will actually change the *color* of one's sound. They may unwittingly display harmonic indifference by performing an entire phrase or movement (or even an entire piece!) using only one sound color, content with simply letting the manifestation of the written pitches generate any and all coloristic changes in the music. Identifying places within a phrase where a subtle change to a complementary sound color can highlight and supplement similar changes in the notation is the sign of a mature artist. It could be one note or a series of notes and can be done at any tempo. A rudimentary application of this type of flavoring can be heard when a jazz player uses a halve valve on a particularly "blue" note. When a performer is responsive to the many shades of color in any given progression of harmony or melody, true artistry can be reached. (Listen to any recording of Sharon Isbin.) It is not a difficult task to make slight changes to one's sound color. However, it does take a high level of sensitivity to the often-subtle changes hidden within a composer's notation to recognize where these changes could and should happen.

There are several works available to brass players that offer ample opportunities to include these various ingredients. Still, one must make a conscious effort to do so. Here are a few particularly fertile compositions.

For trumpet: "Concoctions" by John Cheetham; "Sonata" by Kent Kennan

For French horn: "Laudatio" by Bernard Krol; "Sonata No.2" by Luigi Cherubini

For trombone: "Mippy II" by Leonard Bernstein; "Sonata" by Paul Hindemith

For tuba: "Fantasy" by Malcolm Arnold; "Sonata" by Paul Hindemith

For everybody: Any cello suite by J.S. Bach

The variety with which one can mix and balance these ingredients is infinite. The way *you* mix them not only communicates the depth of your interpretation of the music, but also defines your individual style, showing you to be a mature performing artist or just another crescendoing vibrator. ➤●

Pursuing Goals in a Changing World

Roger Bobo

Some time ago I received a letter from an ambitious high school tuba player who had declared that, in ten years, he was going to be, "hands down, the best tuba player in the world." He already considered himself to be one of the best in his home state and was eager to prove himself. He did not go into detail on how he planned to achieve this goal so I offered him some perspective and a little advice to help in his pursuit.

INGREDIENTS:
Strong desire and commitment, a metronome, a tuner, and a recording device.

SERVES:
Young, aspiring tuba players and their teachers.

It is important that young players are encouraged to pursue their goals. When I was in my early teens, I wrote a letter to William Bell that was much the same as the letter I received from this determined young tuba player. But I wondered if he even knew who William Bell was.

William Bell was the daddy, well, let's change that to granddaddy—or is it great granddaddy?—of all American tubists. You see, the generations of tubists are not the same as regular generations, by my observations through the fifty-four years of my tuba awareness; a tuba generation is about every ten years, and as each of these ten-year tuba generations passes into the next, I am absolutely amazed at how the level of playing and musicianship improves.

About the same time that I wrote that letter to William Bell—it might have been 1950—I was quite interested in sports, particularly swimming as a competitor and track and field as a spectator. It was a great thrill for me to see world records fall and to see the track and swimming times getting faster and faster. One of my heroes in that period was the Australian mile runner Roger Bannister; he was the man whom the world thought would break the seemingly unachievable goal of the "4-minute mile." The world watched as Roger Bannister trained and prepared his strategy for his record-breaking run. Finally, the news came that he had done it. It was a milestone (pun unintended) in track history. Today, a 4-minute mile is still a very good time, but there are hundreds of college and even high school runners that can do it.

When I was a young man, the composer William Kraft wrote a very fine and special piece for me called "Encounters #2." It was considered extremely difficult at that time, and I had heard it said that I was the only person who could play it. If that was true, it was only true for a short time; today you can frequently hear it played by high school and college players. I enjoy very much watching this happen.

But I'm troubled with the thought, "How far can this go?" How fast will it be possible for a man to run a mile? Will we ever see a limit? And in our tuba community, will we continue to excel at the same unbelievable rate that we've seen so far? Of course, I want to believe we can, but when we look at the evolution of more traditional instruments like the violin, for example, we don't see the continuing remarkable growth that is presently visible in the tuba. We see generation after generation of remarkable violinists, but we do not see the expansion of the technical capacities any more. Rather, we see their abilities to express their musicality, their musical souls, and their musical personalities. Today, when we listen to the international competitions for tuba, we begin to hear the same thing, the same growing ability to project a musical atmosphere. Everybody in these competitions has an extraordinary technique; it's the music they make that makes them winners!

The goal to become the world's greatest tubist is a noble one, but there are a few things you should know as you begin this quest. First, please keep in mind that there are other young men and women who have the same goal. It's very much like the Olympics: not every athlete can win a gold medal. However, the performance of these athletes is enhanced by the energy they receive from their competitors. Don't forget that.

There are three pieces of advice I would like to offer to you if you set off on this tuba quest:

1. Become part of the extraordinary tuba community. Read the magazines and books, join the associations, and attend every master class and symposium that you can so that you will know what's happening in the tuba world. And, listen. Listen to every CD, recital, and concert possible. Be aware of every aspect of this tuba world that you are entering.

2. Remember that this tuba community is only a small part of the much bigger and richer musical community. Look beyond the tuba. Look far beyond the tuba world.

3. And, be your own teacher. I'm sure you have a great teacher, but he or she is only your second most important teacher; you are number one! It is fun to think about the things you want in a teacher. Let me start your list for you: good musicianship, intelligence, kindness, wisdom, patience, perseverance, and please don't forget a good sense of humor. Use the learning tools you have: metronome, tuner, and I hope you have and use a MiniDisc so you can play something and instantly hear it back. We hear things differently when we hear ourselves without the horn in our hands!

Just one more thing; the experience you'll have in pursuing your quest for the next ten years will probably be more important in your life than achieving your goal of becoming the greatest tubist. Enjoy this time and I wish you luck in this journey. ➤●

Used here by permission from TubaNews.com and Rogerbobo.com

How Does a Specialty Baker Become a Master Chef? Tips for Horn Players, as They Adapt in Order to Join the Brass Band Movement

Lisa Bontrager

INGREDIENTS:

An alto/tenor horn, an appropriate mouthpiece, an open mind, and an open ear.

SERVES:

Any horn player who wishes to join the Brass Band movement and learn to play the tenor/alto horn.

How does a specialty baker become a master chef? That's a question for all of you French horn players out there who are widening your horizons with the Brass Band movement. I was like 99 percent of the rest of the horn playing world, and became trained by listening to orchestral excepts, while practicing orchestral excerpts, Kopprasch, Maxime-Alponse, and even several bass clef books, as well. I played the descant horn, single Bb horn, natural horn, and every which way on the standard double. I got all of the experience I could get my hands on in brass quintets, woodwind quintets, other chamber music, bands, and orchestras. In other words, I learned how to become the very best baker that I could. And I thought that would be all that was necessary. Then one day, I got a call . . . asking me to work as a chef, with no instructions included! I was asked to play the tenor horn with the Brass Band of Battle Creek. Now, that was about thirteen years ago, and I did not even know what the "tenor horn" was! "Sure, I'll give it a try!"

At the time, the Brass Band of Battle Creek was forging its first several momentous years, and they used a tenor horn section of five French horn transplants. We all worked to grasp the new fingerings, crazy intonation, and even to sink into the jazz swing. It was a tall task! As the Brass Band of Battle Creek has evolved, so has the tenor horn section, now with a section of three players, one on a part, and two coming from Great Britain. The British players are authentic tenor horn players, and they're good. Really good*! I've had the unique privilege to learn from my patient colleagues, so I'll share some cooking tips with my French horn–playing friends out there.

First, get a good instrument. The tenor horn, called the alto horn in the U.S., seems to have inherent intonation problems, like all brass instruments . . . only more so. Third-space C is often sharp, and most are flat below middle C. The best players seem to gravitate towards Boosey and Hawkes/Besson horns and Courtois horns.

And now for a mouthpiece. The tenor horn mouthpiece is much larger than the horn mouthpiece. In fact, it looks more like a smallish tenor trombone mouthpiece. For the first several years, I used my horn mouthpiece with an adapter, to accommodate the much larger leadpipe on the tenor horn. This situation is fraught with problems, and I made the switch to a custom mouthpiece built from the rim of my Holton MC horn mouthpiece and the shank of the tenor horn. Schilke and Moosewood both have made nice mouthpieces for me. I've occasionally played a standard tenor horn mouthpiece, which results in a much nicer sound, but like most of you, I need to keep my day job!

The "trumpet" fingerings might not be a problem for most transplants. If you're like me, you played a marching F horn at some point in life, and I played the trumpet a little, too, but nothing prepared me for the level of technical difficulty in brass band tenor horn parts. Many are orchestral transcriptions and swing charts that have devilish parts. Of course, there is nothing like good old practice. But I found that I just couldn't "feel" the half steps and the keys. So I took one school year and spent 15 minutes most days just playing scales and scale patterns to make the fingerings (and the right hand and the piston valves) feel like second nature. That has made the most significant impact on my ability to sight-read and keep up with the incredible licks and tempos.

Then of course the tenor horn is pitched in E♭, not F, plus the overtones are much farther apart than on the horn. Well, it's kind of fun to not worry much about an entrance on high A! It's quite a lot easier to play accurately, and it only takes a short time to not think about "aiming lower" than usual for the pitch.

Lastly, how does a horn player learn to play jazz? Once again, I was the odd "man" out. Instead of freezing with fear of playing during rests and sounding "ta ta, ta ta," I worked to relax and listen. The playing around me is incredible, and the more I listen and detach myself from the written page, the better it tends to work. As a classical horn player with no jazz training, it's pretty new to *not* read the page, but it really helps.

So, was it worth it trying to learn to become a master chef? Saying "yes" to the tenor horn thirteen years ago has helped me to stretch myself musically and to learn to play another instrument. But the biggest benefit has been meeting all of the fabulous brass players who continue to inspire me beyond belief. And maybe in another thirteen years, I'll have mastered it!

*Recommended listening: *The Voice of the Tenor Horn*, Sheona White, tenor horn; Polyphonic label. It's incredible! ➤

Choosing a Healthy and Complete Start: Is Your Warm-up Nutritious or a Double Espresso Shot Just to Get You Going?

Velvet Brown

In my years of playing and teaching, I have been torn between the phrase "warming up" and "doing a routine." What do I do? What am I asking my students to do? Do they have the same meaning? Do they really accomplish the same goals? These questions need to be investigated by players. A while ago, I had a breakthrough in playing by changing a routine or warm-up to one where the exercises needed to be "practiced" diligently in order to be executed.

During this time period, I asked myself more questions. I realized that I was spending almost half of my daily personal practice time on learning to convincingly and musically execute these exercises. It took time to learn to "perform" them properly, and my attention was focused on always approaching these exercises striving for a high level of musicianship. My ability on the instrument escalated, as did my attention to musical details in all aspects of my playing.

INGREDIENTS:

A musician. Embouchure visualizer. Mouthpiece. Metronome. Keyboard or tuner that plays pitches. Your instrument. Exercises that focus on breathing, mouthpiece playing (buzzing), long tones, flexibility, range, dynamics, phrasing, scales, intervals, articulation, intonation, sight-reading, and agility.

SERVES:

All players that wish to enhance their playing by adding the musician to their routine.
All players that have been just playing their routine without focus.
All players that wish to feel more accomplishment and contentment during and after the warm-up routine.

Sometimes our routine becomes an "à la carte" menu, doing one exercise then another without thinking of how these build together to make a great musical meal. My recipe does not intend to suggest specific exercises, but offers ideas on how to approach some of the exercises that we take for granted on a daily basis and to learn to execute them in a musically satisfying method. In no way are you limited to the ingredients listed above; additions such as a recording device or method books with CD accompaniment will complement the recipe.

First of all, most people begin with a series of breathing exercises. I have noticed that when players do these exercises, most are thinking of only the breathing and not how these breathing exercises will carry forward to the next part of the warm-up routine. Often we think that the breathing is just a series of exercises before the "real" routine starts. So, here is a tip: from the very beginning of the breathing exercises, why not think of your instrument too, and also project your attention to how these exercises and the system of breathing actually reflect the exact method of breathing that should be used when you are playing the mouthpiece and the instrument itself? Also, try thinking about a musical phrase. For instance, if you are breathing in for two counts and then exhaling for eight counts, why not think of a beautiful musical phrase that this could relate to while doing the exercise?

Mouthpiece playing or buzzing is what many consider the next added step. Let's make sure that we are still incorporating the breathing procedures from the breathing exercises. Remember that we continue to "add in" ingredients. Mouthpiece exercises are most effective when accompanied by accurate pitches, such as a keyboard instrument, tuning forks, or tuning machines. It is important to train our ears and embouchures to buzz in tune and to be able to "feel" the note in conjunction with hearing it, for perfect execution. Ideally, try to also visualize the specific pitches on the staff so that the sense of sight is incorporated. Another tip is to make sure that air is the first and major component while mouthpiece buzzing, and to understand that the air that crosses the lips creates the buzzing sound as we "play the mouthpiece." Next we will add the instrument. Are we playing into the instrument with the same great air that we used while playing only the mouthpiece, which incidentally carried forward from our breathing exercises?

Let's add long tones and the other parts. Ask yourself the following questions. What am I thinking about when playing long tones? Am I playing with a beautiful sound? What articulation am I using to start each pitch: air attack or a specified tongued articulation? Where and how does the note end? What dynamic am I going to use? Is there a shape? Am I playing with direction? We focus on the above questions while playing a piece of music or excerpt, but the same focus must accompany our exercises.

When practicing the remaining "ingredients" in your routine, it is important to continue to add on and not to delete previous focus points. No musical phrases are complete without engaging techniques, dynamics, tone, range issues, articulation, etc. The questions above relate to all exercises in general. Even when sight-reading, don't think about just getting the notes and the rhythm; everything should be there. Here is a tip for learning new pieces: Regardless of the tempo, immediately begin to think about the music, phrasing, dynamics, musical contour, and articulation, even in the very slow practice. Too often, we wait until we have learned to play something before we add the "musician."

Last thoughts. It is imperative that the musician is always present during your entire routine or warm-up. We cannot wait to add the musician until we have a piece of music in front of us with a title or a number on top of an etude. All of the routine ingredients are needed when we play solos, etudes, even scales and slurs. We need to shape our routine phrases just as we phrase our most beloved song. Once we get into this habit, the routine will never again be boring, because we are investing our total packages from beginning to end. And each day, don't forget to strive to make all of your playing from the very first buzz to the last blow of the day intensely beautiful and worthwhile. ➤

How to Improve Your Playing Without Practicing (...But I Didn't Say You Should Never Practice!)

John Clark

A pianist or guitarist can practice many, many hours in a day without serious injury. So can a string player, and just about any instrumentalist outside of the brass family. However, brass playing can be somewhat risky to do for more than a couple, three, four hours in a day (since it involves smooshing your lips between a large metal object and your teeth with your very strong arm muscles). Let's say, for example, that you practice three or four hours today, but you still have some free time, and you want to save your chops. You can vastly improve your playing with some of the techniques listed below:

INGREDIENTS:
Your choice of audio player (CD, cassette, 8-track, Victrola . . .).

COOKING TIME:
As long as you like.

SERVES:
Yourself, and all the listeners in the audiences you'll ever play for in your life.

SERVING SUGGESTIONS:
Like leftovers, you can just pop these out of your "fridge" anytime and nuke them.

Instructions:
Listen to a lot of music that you admire. It will rub off. Don't always worry about listening in a technical or analytical way (although that's okay too). Even having it on in the background is effective. But also listen in different ways—for the emotional content, for the tone qualities, the phrasing, articulations, and dynamics. Every piece, solo, and excerpt that you listen to has many facets, and you want to listen to become informed on all of them.

Play the piano or some different instrument or sing. This is somewhat similar to listening, in that it just gives you a different perspective or vantage point on the music. Singing, or solfège, will sharpen your ears, which will help you immensely in playing your instrument.

Read books, articles, interviews, and reviews, and attend master classes. There are so many great texts out there today on every aspect of playing every instrument—you don't have to read a whole book; just skim one until you find something that interests you, and then see how you can apply it to your playing needs. Interviews with great musicians (not just players of your instrument, but any artists, composers, conductors—even critics) can be very inspiring. Master classes are a great way to learn. Whether you are the master, student, or spectator, you will invariably learn a lot.

Sit and think about your playing. Assess it from time to time. See where you think you are, where you need to be, and how you think you can get there. This might sound easy, but it's not. Henry Ford once said, "Thinking is the hardest work there is, which is probably the reason why so few engage in it."

Work on memorizing music. You don't need your horn to do this; you can do it while you're on a boring bus ride or trying to get to sleep at night. It can actually be a great cure for insomnia. The ability to play a piece from memory actually makes it much easier to play; your brain isn't busy looking at the page of music and processing the information. You're able to focus more on the music and whatever physical issues you may have to deal with.

Study any kind of discipline that will help calm your mind and strengthen your body— yoga, tai chi, martial arts. Any kind of aerobic exercise is great; even walking is better than nothing. These disciplines will give you more power and control, since they help to integrate your mental and physical faculties. Breathing exercises are extremely useful, and you can do them anywhere for any amount of time you feel like devoting to them.

Keep your instrument in top shape. Why make things more difficult with sticky valves, leaks, and green slime in your slides? First of all, keep it clean and lubricated, but also stay informed on various improvements that are being made.

Talk about it. Your friends and colleagues have interesting things to say. Ask their opinions and thoughts about all aspects of playing and music. Share your ideas with them. You may find that you had a wrong idea about something, or you'll get confirmation of your own ideas. Either way, you win!

One last thought to complete the preparation of this recipe: These techniques are useful when you are too tired physically to continue practicing, but they also apply when you are too tired mentally, or are bored with your routine. If you have just been practicing long tones and scales for three hours, you need inspiration. It's out there; it's all around you, so go find something that will help you clarify your goals and keep you motivated! ➤●

Some Observations on Respiration

Dale Clevenger

Shortly after arriving in Chicago—forty years ago, alas, forty wondrous years, February 6, 1966—I was visiting in Arnold Jacobs' home along with his first cousin, Joseph Singer. We had enjoyed a lovely dinner prepared by Arnie's wife, Gizzy. After dinner Joe and I had our lung capacities measured. Joe's was about four liters and mine was six liters. I was twenty-five years old. In the ensuing years, for the rest of Jake's career, he and I had dozens of conversations back stage in many concert halls throughout the world about breathing (respiration). For years I have used the information I learned from Jake, and talked about proper breathing to all my students. I have stressed taking full, deep, yoga-like, inspired breaths of air as a "normal" function in our profession.

While I have always tried to practice what Jake and I preached for years, it is lately that I have really been forced to re-examine this whole, extremely vital subject of respiration. Because recently, I discovered that I now possess *four* liters of air and not the *six* liters, with which I began this wonderful venture. Jake always maintained that improper use of a brass player's respiration, breathing, lungs, wind is the *basis*, the *core*, the *primary physical* (not mental!) *problem*, and the *reason* for the vast majority of brass player's demise or necessary departure from the stage or from successful performance.

There are, of course, notable exceptions—people who have used wind properly throughout their careers. The most famous of these is Adolph "Bud" Herseth, who served for fifty-three years as principal trumpet in the Chicago Symphony Orchestra. But, in the course of my years with Arnold Jacobs (another famous exception, by the way), hundreds of brass and woodwind players and singers came in a steady flow to Chicago to see Jake. He saved countless careers by discovering and pointing out respiration deficiencies, suggesting ways of turning negatives into positives, and changing the deficient into efficient and successful performers.

INGREDIENTS:
A realistic expectation for the future. A commitment to preparing oneself for the longevity.

SERVES:
All wind and brass players.

What's my point?
Beginners, students, amateurs, teachers, and professional brass players and musicians, I freely give this information—even more, *criteria*—for success. Like me and all brass players

who are aging, we are also *losing* air capacity as we age. If we do not recognize this fact and actively remember to use *what* air/wind/fuel capacity we have as efficiently and effectively as humanly possible, we will soon join the ranks of the early retirees. (I am not speaking of those who choose to stop or have to stop playing for personal or other physical reasons. I am speaking first to *myself* and then to all who want to play and perform as long as physically possible and as long as we enjoy and have fun performing.)

Remember: breathe full, deep, yawn-like, and inspired intakes of air and then use it as efficiently and effectively as possible. Some things to assist us in this process are:

1. Pretend you are diving or going under water in order to swim quite a distance. The breath you would take would not be a small, "half-hearted" one.
2. You would not be concerned in the least about how much your thoracic (chest) cavity moves.
3. The comfort level of this extreme breathing movement is very different from the "normal" daily breathing, which is a natural reflex activity. The physical sensation of a deep breath may seem at first uncomfortable and unnatural . . . it is, and this is okay.
4. As a runner, exerciser, or sportsperson is panting greatly at the end of a race, game, exercise routine, or even a marathon, so we must thoughtfully and in a calculated and purposeful way simulate this respiration of athletes.
5. Another analogy of breathing used by Mr. Jacobs is a "fright and flight" response. This is a psychological term that describes an instinctive, life-saving breath.
6. Teachers who advocate nonmovement of certain areas of the upper body while breathing are really doing a disservice to the student. Every person moves differently while breathing deeply. Movement is a result of breathing fully, not a criteria of how to breathe.
7. Under the stress of a lesson, rehearsal, audition, or performance, all brass players are likely to forget to breathe deeply enough to perform at optimum level. Our nerves or fear factor (negative terminology), which I refer to as anxiety, concern, or care (more positive terminology), under stress, often cause us to breathe too shallow, with not nearly enough fuel to function comfortably. Those of us who are aging will certainly notice this syndrome sooner or later—alas, sometimes too late!
8. We must, particularly in our practice of quality tones (long tones), scales, etudes, and everything musical, make deep breathing a *habit*. For the sake of our career, we have no choice in this most important *physical* part of playing a brass or wind instrument but to breathe as if our careers depend on it . . . and they do! ➤●

Cooking in High Altitudes: Whirled Peas, or How to Spread Peace as a Brass Player

Abbie Conant

(These peas can be spread on anything!)

INGREDIENTS:
Homegrown peas, conscious brass players, imagination, vision, willingness, and will.

SERVES:
All humanity.

Why do you do what you do? Do you really understand your motivations? Are you in love with music or with yourself? Can we as brass players make our moves toward more peace in the world? As the song says, "Let it begin with me." How do we begin?

By being peaceful.

Helpful hint: When you blame others, you give up your power to change. You become stuck and miserable. Forgive yourself, forgive everyone else, and then focus on your most inspiring vision of what you want your life to be and mean. Maybe you have noticed that you are happiest when you are pursuing worthwhile, challenging goals that really cause you to grow and expand in every way.

As a soloist:
Consciously intend to send out peace, kindness, positive energy—blessings, if you will—as part of your sound. Stay up in the high altitudes of your mind. Send out the most inspired thoughts and feelings you possibly can. Combined with excellent musical preparation, you are then able to truly give your best. The audience will definitely hear it on some level and respond in kind. Peace will be magnified.

As an ensemble member:
Same as above, but don't forget to send out peace to your colleagues. Support them not only as a trained musician but also as another human being. Help them to sound good by bending the intonation a little if you have to, for example, or by imitating their articulation if it doesn't harm the sound of the whole ensemble. Agree with them musically and mentally. See if you can honestly wish them well—if not, fake it until it becomes real. If you can do this for rehearsals and concerts, you will be able to do it outside of the music world, as well.

This is not to say that you need to be a doormat or a pushover. Stand behind your musical opinions but don't be attached to them to the point of ugly conflict. They are, after all, only opinions and every one has at least one. Ask yourself if insisting on your interpretation is worth sacrificing your own and probably everyone else's inner peace.

As a teacher:
If a student doesn't appear to be making progress, consider creating an atmosphere of peace and support for them, and nothing else. Stop pushing them in every way. Stop and really listen to who they are and where they are coming from. Give up. You may have missed something while you were trying to get them to understand your teachings. Inevitably they will communicate how they need to learn . . . how they need to be treated. Sometimes as teachers, we are so intent on getting the student to be able to develop certain skills that we miss important cues that indicate a short circuit in our mutual communication flow. Visualize and feel that the student is in your heart, that you want the very best for them in their playing, and recognize how it integrates into their whole life. They will relax and be more receptive if you can do this with utter sincerity.

Throw all these ideas together inside your head and let them soak in for several weeks or months before tossing out. They get much better with age. Have some with every practice session, rehearsal, and concert. Share them with friends, enemies, and strangers, and you will never run out of true sustenance. Your sound will improve, your happiness will grow, you will become more relaxed, and you just might start a quiet and musically satisfying revolution.

Enjoy spreading "whirled peas" on everything and everybody! ➦

Attention Trumpet Players: Superchops in Just 8 Minutes a Day

Jeffrey Curnow

INGREDIENTS:
A daily routine. Your instrument. Warm water.

SERVES:
All trumpet players.

Right. You wish. Now I know what you're thinking—you're thinking that if this is another one of those *"quit looking for a quick fix, stop all your whining and get back into the practice room"* articles, you're going to soak your horn in Blue Juice and fire it out of a circus cannon. Well, hold on. You might be pleasantly surprised. Okay, I'll admit that the title was a cruel trick, but I was aiming to attract readers just like you—the trumpeter who's looking for more efficient ways to get better, faster.

I'm convinced that we trumpeters *are* what we practice on a daily basis. We start each day with our daily routines, and those routines form what we can and can't do on the instrument. If you want to change your playing for the better, make some adjustments to that routine. Within a short time—or, in some cases, immediately—you're a better player. (I should also mention that it's a good idea that you actually *have* a daily routine to which to add these. If you don't have a daily routine, look for my next article entitled "What Arban Didn't Tell You: Complete Warm-up in 3 Minutes or Less!" Right. You wish.)

The following are a few "adjustments" that can quickly and simply improve your trumpet playing. The most difficult aspect of these "quick fix tips" is remembering to do them every single time you play.

The first tip deals with your posture. Yes, your mother was right when she told you to sit up straight. Improving your posture, both while standing and sitting, can instantly improve your trumpet playing. Singers have understood the importance of posture for over a century now, so it's past time for us trumpeters to all jump on the bandwagon. Just try it. Sit on the edge of your chair with your feet planted flat on the floor and your back straight. From the very first time you try it, you'll immediately notice how much easier it is to both support your sound and to take that all-important breath before you make a sound. The byproduct of this support and breathing efficiency is a richer, more relaxed tone.

Now that your posture is in place and it's easier to take a breath, it's time to talk air. You want to know just how important air is to trumpet playing? Try making a sound on the instrument without it! If you master your management of the air stream, you will be better prepared to master playing the trumpet. Think of the air being to the trumpet what the bow is to the violin. You want to make sure you're using a full bow every time you play so that you achieve the fullest sound and the greatest agility in your performance. The easiest way to achieve this "full bow" effect on a trumpet is to simply take a big breath before you play. This will immediately improve sound, articulation, and perhaps even range and endurance. Just with a big breath. It sounds easy, but an "easy breath" would be the kind of breath you take while lying on the couch watching Monday night football. That's easy.

Taking a full breath requires a bit more effort and that's where it becomes difficult. Remembering to take the full breath *every single time* becomes a challenge, as well. Keep in mind that what I mean by a full breath is not a *desperate* breath, but just a relaxed breath that comfortably fills your lungs. Even for those soft passages, a full breath for *pianissimo* playing will give your tone a rich core and will boost response. So think about the breath you take before you play the very first note of the day and remember to do it for every single note or phrase thereafter. Your lips will thank you for it.

The next tip has to do with your **valves.** You may have the world's fastest fingers, but you still need to make sure the valves go all the way up and all the way down, firmly and with rhythmic conviction. This will immediately improve your playing on a couple of fronts. First, quick and complete valve action will route the vibrating air stream throughout the different lengths of tubing more efficiently—this works wonders in soft passages. Second, it will improve the rhythm in slurred passages (like the ones found in Stravinsky's "Ballerina's Dance" from *Petroushka*.)

And finally, my last quick fix tip may seem a bit silly to you but, trust me, it can make a huge difference in your practice and performance. **Keep your horn clean!** I can't tell you the number of times a student has come to me with range, endurance, or sound problems and I've found an herb garden growing in their leadpipe. All that toxic sludge stuck throughout the horn will undoubtedly change its response, sound, and resistance and, at times, really interfere with your progress—not to mention eventually eat away at the inside of the instrument. Taking apart the horn and cleaning it can be very time consuming, but well worth the time and effort.

Here's a quick and easy way to keep it clean between full cleanings:

Every two weeks (or more often, if you're the type to eat and practice at the same time), blow a mouthful of warm water through the mouthpiece and instrument while holding all the valves down. Doing this two or three times will clean out a large percentage of the crud. This by no means is a substitute for a good, complete cleaning but, if done regularly between full cleanings, will keep your horn blowing as freely as the day you bought it.

There you have it: some tips for you quick-fix fanatics. And you thought this article was going to be depressing! Even the most experienced players remind themselves of these important strategies on a regular basis—they're one-size-fits-all. So next time you head for the practice room, think about your posture, air, and fingers, and instantly make some changes in your playing for the better. (And don't forget to pull out the tuning slide and see if any light gets through that leadpipe.) ➤

Managing a Section of Nineteen

Kurt Dupuis

Human nature dictates that everyone wants to feel appreciated, so how do you manage the musical ego of a large section without compromising its musical integrity? Doing so wisely may in fact enhance the overall musical product as well as increase its morale.

INGREDIENTS:

Conductors, principal players, and section leaders: know your personnel's strengths and weaknesses.

Principal players: prolong your career while enhancing that of your section.

Section players: take pride that your role is crucial to the success of the ensemble.

SERVES:

Conductors, principal players, section leaders, and members of large band sections.

As principal trumpet of a large section of nineteen, getting everyone their "touches" or "minutes," as they say in the sports world, can be a challenge. As a principal player, the demands of the job can be brutal. Our organization has a seven-week annual concert tour with only three days off during that span. When not on tour, there are a variety of commitments that occur. Some include: marching funerals at Arlington National Cemetery; weekly band, orchestral, or chamber music concerts; official events at the White House, including State Dinners.

I have been a section player as well as a principal player and have a good understanding of the ego involved in both positions. Prior to being named principal trumpet, I was a member of a section with no rotation and often wondered if one could work. So after being named principal, I decided to implement some form of rotation. Knowing that I work with some of the most talented players in the country, the hardest part would be figuring out how to utilize everyone without jeopardizing the musical consistency of the section. After an assessment of the section, the goal was to showcase the strengths of each player while minimizing the wear and tear that will occur over the career of a band trumpeter.

For a principal player, it is important to understand one's limitations. It is tempting at times to take on the full load of a concert on any given night. While okay in the short term, there is a long-term downside. Physical burnout may occur and a career could be shortened as a result. I have found that leaving the stage and letting my peers have a go at it makes my job more manageable long term and has a positive effect on the morale of the section. Conductors are used to seeing and hearing their principal players. In order to build trust using different personnel, it is vital that you know players' strengths and weaknesses and carefully choose pieces for them to shine. Making wrong decisions in this area can be devastating to a player's confidence.

Since it is my belief that sports and music have many similarities, here are some professional sports analogies. All championship sports teams have common characteristics. They have good leadership, they have "go to" and "role" players, and they all have good team depth. In basketball you have the "sixth man;" defensive, rebounding, and three-point specialists. In football, you have kickers, special teams, pass, rush, and kick return specialists, as well as two different styles of running backs. In baseball, you have a pitching staff comprised of starters, middle relief, and closers. There are also pinch runners, pinch hitters, and defensive specialists.

Much the same can be said of a well-built musical section. How you utilize everyone's unique talents takes much time, consideration, and patience. In the trumpet/cornet section of my organization, everyone contributes. There are principals, assistant principals, section players, and lead and jazz specialists. Some feel comfortable playing piccolo trumpet, or lead in a big band, while others excel in areas such as chamber settings or soloing in front of a jazz combo. There are even administrative issues such as building music folders, ordering musical supplies, scheduling vacations, etc. that are delegated amongst our section. While it's not a computer model in which everyone plays first a set amount of times, it is a common-sense approach that aims to get everyone involved in their most confident capacity.

Lastly, I know from my own experience that sitting next to a professional or principal player will give you an immense amount of feedback that you may not otherwise get. Rotating players up and down in a section helps to give that experience. The drawback in rotating too frequently is a possible lack of cohesiveness. Careful consideration of assignments as well as patience for individuals to grow in their "roles" will in the long run lead to a "deep" section.

Ask any principal player and he or she will tell you that having a strong section to rely on makes life much easier. For those of you who feel uninspired by playing section parts, just remember there are many people making a good living today by doing just that. There is an art to playing inner parts. You must have a great ear and the ability to instantly adjust to pitch. You must have as much command of your instrument as the principal and have incredible musical instincts to follow what's going on around you. And as important as a person's musical qualities is his or her personality. It is satisfying to know I will be spending much of my life performing with some of the most supportive and nicest individuals I've ever met.

Good luck with mixing up your own ingredients and creating your own unique recipe for success.

Eight-Layer Trom-"Bone-In"-tonation Supreme

Peter Ellefson

This recipe is intended to aid in the improvement of accurate slide technique by clarifying, emphasizing, and reinforcing the difference between half steps and whole steps.

The design of the slide trombone offers the player an opportunity to play perfectly in tune at all times. Unfortunately, along with the ability to play perfectly in tune comes the possibility of playing completely out of tune. Although no one plays perfectly in tune all of the time, some have more success than others. Accurate intonation is a lifelong pursuit for the conscientious trombonist.

Accurate intonation is a combination of a good sound, keen intervallic sense, and instantaneous adjustment. A tuner is a valuable tool but not nearly as valuable as a well-trained ear. Although the tuner is one of the tools in the intonation toolbox, well-schooled trombonists understand and are sensitive to the additional subtleties of harmonic intonation. Use the tuner as only a point of reference.

One particularly difficult passage involves going from fourth position to first position with one note in between. For example, playing D–E–F in a rapid manner as part of a musical passage. The tendency I see in many students (and also in myself) is to carelessly split the difference between fourth position and first position, which produces a quite flat E. To fix this, the player must concentrate on keeping the E high enough by playing a true second-position E. The same would apply for keeping the E-flat low, if the same passage contained an E-flat.

Likewise, the same concept would need to be applied in all registers and all passages to attain a high degree of pitch accuracy. It is merely a matter of paying attention. A recorder with half-speed playback capabilities is a very valuable tool in building accurate intonation. Being aware of the tendency is the first step toward correcting it. This recipe will help the player develop a new appreciation for the higher degree of clarity that precise slide technique produces.

INGREDIENTS:
Trombone with slide in good working order
Mouthpiece
Electronic tuner
Concentration
10–15 minutes daily

SERVES:
All trombonists.

To prepare this highly beneficial dish, examine the chart below:

Layer	Step Formula	Sample Ingredients
1	H–H–H	F–E–E♭–D
2	H–H–W	F–E–E♭–D♭
3	H–W–H	F–E–D–D♭
4	H–W–W	F–E–D–C
5	W–H–H	F–E♭–D–D♭
6	W–H–W	F–E♭–D–C
7	W–W–H	F–E♭–D♭–C
8	W–W–W	F–E♭–D♭–C♭

H = Half-step W = Whole-step

Procedure:

Use an electronic tuner to get the instrument as close to "in tune" as possible.

For each of the above layers, apply the following rhythmic patterns:

- Repeat each pitch four times descending then ascending, returning to the first note. Repeat the pattern twice.
- Repeat each note twice. Repeat the pattern three times.
- One note per pitch, repeating the pattern four times.

Once the pattern of the layer is memorized, observe the slide to make certain that the notes are in the same location ascending as they were descending. Combine visual and aural senses to zero-in on crystal clear accuracy. After comfort is gained, increasing the tempo will provide the added benefit of working on clear articulation (another bane of the trombonist's existence).

Tasty variances include spicing up the recipe by applying various predetermined articulations and dynamics, and executing the patterns in all registers.

After a very short time a heightened awareness of half-step, whole-step intonation will result, which will be healthy and beneficial to all. ➤●

Superior CAFÉ: Control, Accuracy, Flexibility, Endurance

Laurie Frink

A Progressive Practice Routine

INGREDIENTS:
Intermediate trumpet player. Practice time/space.

PREPARATION TIME:
20–40 minutes, 6x/week for 1–50 years. (Actual time may vary according to age level, interest, and motivation of player.)

YIELD:
Upon completion of this four-week course of practice, the conscientious player will obtain Superior CAFÉ . . . Control, Accuracy, Flexibility, and Endurance.

SERVES:
Every ensemble with which the player is involved.

Week 1

Ingredient 1: "Long Setting"
Practice of the following study will stabilize the embouchure and allow it to come into focus before adding motion or other challenges. It is adapted from Carmine Caruso's original six-note exercise. It should be played without removing the mouthpiece from the lips and is referred to as a "long setting" exercise. All breaths are taken through the nose, leaving the embouchure unbroken. This exercise teaches the lips to move from one note to the next *inside* the mouthpiece. Long-setting practice reduces extraneous motion when moving between registers, and automatically increases endurance and accuracy.

Ingredient 2: Flexibility

Flexibility is the most fundamental trumpet skill. Maintaining a steady air stream is necessary for good flexibility, and flexibility studies in turn develop a consistent air stream.

Ingredient 3: Chromatic Displacement

This study is designed to connect the registers, resulting in freer movement throughout the entire range of the instrument. Play each exercise three times, beginning at the slow tempo and doubling the tempo each time you repeat the study.

Week 2

Ingredient 1: "Long Setting"

Continue to practice Ingredient 1 from Week 1.

Ingredient 2: Flexibility

Continue to practice Ingredient 2 from Week 1 with the following additions:

Ingredient 3: Chromatic Displacement

Continue to practice Ingredient 3 from Week 1 with the following addition:

Week 3

Ingredient 1: "Long Setting"

Add a repeat to this exercise.

Ingredient 2: Flexibility

Continue to practice Ingredient 2 from Weeks 1 and 2 with the following additions:

Ingredient 3: Chromatic Displacement

Continue to practice Ingredient 3 from Weeks 1 and 2 with the following addition:

Week 4

Ingredient 1: "Long Setting"
Continue to practice with repeat.

Ingredient 2: Flexibility
Continue to practice Ingredient 2 from Weeks 1, 2, and 3 with the following additions:

Ingredient 3: Chromatic Displacement
Continue to practice Ingredient 3 from Weeks 1, 2, and 3 with the following addition:

Suggested accompaniments:

"Twenty-SEVEN Groups of Exercises for Cornet and Trumpet," by Earl D. Irons

"Lip Flexibilities for all Brass Instruments," by Bai Lin

Any etude book written by Sigmund Hering

This recipe was excerpted from "Flexus"–Trumpet Calisthenics for the Modern Improvisor by Laurie Frink and John McNeil, published by Omnitone Press. Used by permission.

Writing for Brass Quintet

Jack Gale

INGREDIENTS:
Knowledge of the natural range of the instruments you're writing for
An understanding of harmony
A familiarity with the genre in which you are writing
Manuscript paper and pencil (or a computer, notation software, and printer)

SERVES:
Anyone who wants to write for brass chamber groups.

Transcription

The principles of brass quintet arranging and orchestration are not dissimilar to those involved in *all* small ensemble writing. One very good way to learn arranging and orchestration is by transcribing a quality piece of four- or five-line music.

A Bach chorale is ideal for this purpose. The four parts can be assigned to the two trumpets, horn, and trombone (optionally doubled an octave lower by the tuba or bass trombone). Another approach could be to start with any four instruments and shift between various other combinations of four. For example, if there are lower passages, they can be scored for trumpet, horn, trombone, and tuba, higher passages for two trumpets, horn, and trombone, etc. Two important rules: Don't change any notes (this music is not improvable) and keep each instrument in its comfortable range.

Similarly, learning linear writing can be aided by transcribing a Bach fugue. Again, the lines need to be exactly as written and each instrument should be kept in its natural range. One trick is to develop a three-part version with the basic lines and harmonies in place. Then develop a five-part version and use the addition of the other instruments to create opportunities for rests, adding important missing harmony notes and covering any needed subordinate phrases.

Music with more than four or five original lines needs to be somewhat arranged, even in transcription. A piano piece or an orchestral selection may require a certain amount of judgment. Decide what the key lines are and which harmonies are essential to the effect of the original music. In other words, determine which notes can be left out without harming the character of the composition.

Arranging

Concert pieces can be developed by arranging, rather than simply transcribing, existing music. This approach allows altering harmonies and rhythms, creating new counterlines and developing themes as seems appropriate. Here many kinds of voicings are possible since the precise lines in the original composition are no longer written in stone.

A solid understanding of harmony and voicings is necessary to do an interesting arrangement of a standard classical theme or pop tune. Again, every instrument should be kept within its natural range. Each horn can be given the melody (or the lead).

Other variations in texture can be achieved by using pairs of instruments in harmony, unison, or octaves. Doublings can be very effective. Total group unison or octaves can also work well. Various combinations of three or four of the horns can provide rest and give the impression of more instruments.

Full five-part writing can work in wide or in close harmony and even in clusters. One way to get a big sound out of any small ensemble, especially a brass group, is to build a chord up from a low, open fifth or tenth interval in the bottom two voices, and fill in the other two harmony parts between these and the top note in Trumpet 1. In contrast, close voicings can achieve a very thick rich quality. Occasionally, even a cluster of four or five notes within one octave can produce a powerful sound. A close chord or a cluster is also a good starting point for a series of chords in which the bottom and top lines move in opposite directions and wind up in a wide open voicing (or vice versa).

Like a string quartet or a woodwind quintet, a brass quintet can create the impression of a full orchestra. Of course, it is better to save the full *tuttis* for climaxes and bigger sections and to be sure to include lighter voicings, solos, and duets etc., throughout to provide contrast with the wider and fuller passages.

Composition

Creating a composition is far easier in terms of harmony and voicings. Unlike an arranger or transcriber, a composer can write any notes or lines he or she chooses. Presumably the music has been conceived for five brass so there should be no problems of missing themes or notes, and no incomplete chords.

There are really very few rules for compositional orchestration, especially for music in a contemporary or dissonant mode. Unconventional harmonies, unfamiliar rhythms, and long silences are all quite acceptable. Awkward passages or out-of-range notes can actually be very effective in a "modern" composition, and there is less need to worry about the listener failing to hear certain expected harmonic elements as they might in a more familiar or conventional piece.

The most basic decision to make is whether to create a chamber piece with a traditional brass quintet sound or to try to build a composition that reflects a more orchestral concept.

Whichever approach is taken, it is important to realize the inherent potential of all five instruments and make sure each of the parts is meaningful.

Jazz and Pop Arrangements

Arranging nonclassical music presents a few special problems. The most challenging is the absence of a rhythm section. Pop and jazz music rely greatly on the input of piano, bass, guitar, drums, and other rhythm instruments.

A piano or guitar, for example, can add important but subtle harmonic and rhythmic elements. The presence of an occasional piano chord (however simple or complex) can say a great deal about both the feel and the harmony of the music, perhaps without even being consciously noticed by the listener. A few brass instruments might come close to creating this effect but then they may not be available for other important ensemble functions in the arrangement.

No brass instrument can emulate the sound or feel of a snare drum, bass drum, cymbal, or most other percussion instruments. Partly because the sounds are pitch neutral, a rhythm pattern performed on a percussion instrument can be far more simply effective and inconspicuous than a similar figure played on a brass instrument.

Replacing a jazz or rock bass is a bit more workable, but even the common device of having a tuba or bass trombone emulate a walking bass is not always completely effective and requires additional skill, endurance, and breath control on the part of the player.

One way to address the absence of a rhythm section is to simply infuse as much rhythm as possible into the harmonic and linear elements themselves. This may mean adjusting some of the rhythms in the inside lines so that there are fewer empty beats. A familiarity with standard jazz and rock rhythmic figuration is definitely worth developing in order to learn to give the rhythm section-less quintet a more authentic feel.

A grasp of modern jazz and pop harmony is also important in order to add chordal interest and authenticity to contemporary nonclassical arrangements. The more rhythms that can be combined with harmonic elements, the more effectively both can be enhanced without making the result sound too "busy."

A Few General Rules

Brass instruments can be tiring and any arrangement will sound better if each player has enough rest during the piece. The earlier mentioned trick of writing a preliminary arrangement for three or four horns is great for finding places for players to rest. If the piece works with fewer voices, the others can then be added for additional color and weight but also to replace some of the notes in the original voices, so that all of the players can be given some rest.

Save the full five-part, big-sounding chords for climaxes, endings, and other high-profile passages, both as an aid to endurance and to give the music shape and forward motion.

It is important to make each part interesting. Also, if everyone can be featured occasionally, even for only a phrase or two, the arrangement will be more enjoyable to listen to and more fun to play. Giving a player a beat or two of rest before a solo or featured line is also valuable.

Learning to write brass quintet arrangements can be useful as a musical exercise, and as a way to expand a group's repertoire and create unique material for special concerts.

Singing Approach to Ear Training for Jazz Improvisation

Wycliffe Gordon

INGREDIENTS:
Music for one song: "All The Things You Are"
Primary recording device
Secondary recording device (4-track recorder may be substituted)
Metronome (w/batteries)
Chromatic musical instrument
Piano
Pitch pipe (optional)

SERVES:
All musicians.

ADDITIONAL CATEGORIES AND SONG TITLES:
Blues: "Blue Monk," "Sonnymoon for Two," etc. . . .
Ballad: "I Can't Get Started," "For All We Know," etc. . . .
32-bar song form: "How High the Moon," "Donna Lee," etc. . . .

Instructions:
1. Set the metronome at quarter note = 60–80 beats per minute. Turn metronome on and operate at this tempo until step 7 of session.
2. Activate your recording device.
3. Play the melody to "All The Things You Are." Shut off recording device and rewind. (Listen once to make sure all notes are correct and in tune. Re-record if necessary for accuracy.) Listen to the recording several times while following the chart. Then attempt to sing the melody from memory. Repeat several times or as needed to complete memorization process.
4. Play and record the tonic of the chords (also called the root), giving each note the value suggested by the changes (whole and half notes, mostly). Listen to this recording a few times while reading chart, then sing the tonic of chords along with the recording, then without. Repeat as needed to memorize.
5. Play the chord changes on the piano and record for three choruses. Listen to this recording at least three times to "internalize" the sound of the changes. (This is where the development of the harmonic hearing comes in). Begin to sing the melody with the recording of the harmony playing. Repeat three times, then sing the roots of the chords along with the recording of the harmony playing three times also.

6. At the piano, play quarter notes of broken chords for each measure, spelled out from the tonic to the 7th of each chord (root position). This segment should be done in eight measures at a time. (i.e., Fmin7 = F–A♭–C–E♭)

Ex.: Section 1: F–A♭–C–E♭/B♭–D♭–F–A♭/E♭–G–B♭–D♭/A♭–C–E♭–G/D♭–F–A♭–C/ G–B–D–F/C–E–G–B/C–E–G–B.

Play and record the eight bars in succession four times—two times without sustain pedal and two times with sustain pedal—to hear how the chords are constructed. After recording, listen to this recording three times, then attempt to sing the chord pitches along with the recording. Record your voice singing the chord pitches, then listen to the recording, checking for accuracy in pitch and intonation. This will really help with hearing the foundation of the chord changes, creating a true sense and understanding of the "sound" from which the improvisation will take place.

7. You are now set to "hear" and "play" through the changes. Set your metronome at a tempo close to the suggested one for the composition (quarter note = 126–168-ish). Record the chord progression of "All The Things You Are" in its entirety at the chosen tempo, and play through for three choruses. Rewind device and press Play. Sing the melody through with the recording for the first chorus. On choruses 2 and 3, follow your "ear" and sing what you naturally "hear" over the changes, preferably in two-bar phrases to begin with.

After doing this a few times with the recording, employ your secondary recording device and play the first while singing along and recording. Try this for a couple of choruses and record each. Take a 30-minute break from music, then sit and listen to recording for 30 minutes. Try to retain what you heard and maybe notate what you sang. This is what and how you naturally hear.

8. You are now set with a method for developing improvisatory ideas over familiar songs, and have a technique from which to learn new tunes.

9. To further develop this ear training, continue to utilize this concept on other compositions and categories of music (ballads, blues, and 32-bar songs).

10. To further develop your ability to improvise, begin practicing songs that offer more of a challenge melodically and harmonically (ex.: *"Donna Lee," "Ornithology," "Blues for Alice"*) and play/sing through everything utilizing the aforementioned steps 1–7. Where it is applicable, learn the words to songs (especially ballads).

11. Sing everything, everything, everything! It is the voice that gives way to the development of one's "voice" on any instrument. ➡

Vibrato for the Tuba?

James Gourlay

INGREDIENTS:
Tuba, metronome, tuner (optional), lots of air (it's free after all), and patience!

SERVES:
All tubists and other low brass players.

For many, the very idea of playing with vibrato on the tuba is like committing the ultimate *faux pas*, but like all things in life, it's just a matter of taste. Certainly, if you are playing solo repertoire that's lyrical and expressive, you might choose to embellish your sound a little, or even a lot, depending on the message you want to communicate to your listeners. Lots of top tuba soloists agree with me too! But, if you don't use vibrato now and would like to, how can you learn how to do it? When should you use it and, perhaps more importantly, when shouldn't you use it? Let's have a look.

Repertoire
What we play can be divided into three distinct categories: 1) orchestral, 2) band and large ensemble playing, and chamber music (brass quintets and other small ensembles), and 3) solo playing.

Playing in an orchestra or band usually doesn't call for a lot of vibrato, as normally we have to provide a strong foundation to the orchestra's tuning. Vibrato at the bottom of a chord, particularly one that changes the pitch, could prove to be unsettling. We also have to play in a section with the trombones, and the golden rule here is: if they don't use vibrato, we don't either.

There are times though, even in an orchestra, where the tuba plays with other instrumental groups, such as the 'cellos and double basses, which do use vibrato. For me, the rule here is: if they are using it, I might too!

Even so, you'll have to think about the origins of the music you are playing, the nature of the passage, and the type of the vibrato to use. (Yes, there's more than one type!)

Let's look at two musical examples. The first is an extract from Prokofiev's ballet *Romeo and Juliet*. It's a very lyrical passage played with the double basses. The music is very expressive and it's Russian! Just listen to a Russian orchestra play, and hear why this is important. All the brass are using vibrato.

S. Prokofiev *Romeo and Juliette*

The second example is the famous "solo" from the overture to *Die Meistersinger von Nürnberg* by Richard Wagner. It's not a really a solo, as the double basses play along too, but it is pretty exposed *and* it's always on most audition lists. This is probably one to play without vibrato, as German music doesn't usually require it. Listen to recordings of German orchestras and you'll hear a big difference between them and American, French, and British orchestras. And that's the interesting thing: each major musical region has its own style of playing and its own take on the vibrato question, so try to learn what those differences are and assimilate them into your own playing.

Vibrato: Two Basic Types

In solo playing or in the brass ensemble, the tuba player has a lot more freedom. It's here perhaps that playing with vibrato becomes more important. Listen to great singers, flute, or string players, and it quickly becomes apparent that they all use vibrato. In singing, it seems the most natural thing to do, so why not on the tuba? Euphonium players have been doing it for years. Here's how we can learn and practice it.

Pulsation or Air Vibrato

The exercise below will help you make a pulsation, or air, vibrato. Take a very deep breath, start the notes with a breath attack, then without breaking the air stream or sound, make the rhythms shown. "Say" the syllables shown in the exercise, pushing the air with your diaphragm and making those accents quite strong. Don't make any gaps between the notes. Keeping in rhythm, you'll notice that you are getting faster as you proceed through the exercise. When it becomes easy to maintain the faster rhythms (and it will, if you keep at it!) nudge the metronome mark up. Before you know it, you're making vibrato. Eventually, try this on every note of your instrument, gradually increasing the tempo.

Now this type of rhythmic pulse can get pretty predictable, so why not switch from eighths to tuplets and back? Try the exercise below. It'll help you incorporate uneven rhythms into your pulse vibrato, which in turn will help you to become *natural.* Don't just stick to these rhythms; make up a few of your own.

Pitch Vibrato

Let's look now at another type of vibrato. This one involves changing the pitch, slightly bending it away from the core note and bringing it back again. Take a very deep breath before each repetition as you'll need lots of air! Commencing with a middle-register, no-valve note (this exercise is written for the F tuba, but you can transpose it to fit all instruments), try to bend the pitch down as far as it will go, without valves, *whilst keeping an excellent tone quality.* Then return to the original pitch. Drop your jaw slightly to effect the change and increase the air stream. Try to "say" AY (as in "day") and then slowly drop the jaw to "say" AWE (as in "awesome" . . . you will be!). The pitch should fall considerably.

Follow the rhythmic patterns as accurately as possible, and again, when the exercise becomes easy to play at the marked metronome mark, increase the speed. Try this, too, on every note you can play. This exercise is really useful for intonation, sound control, and a whole host of other great things. You can use a tuner as a pitch reference, but I just use my ears!

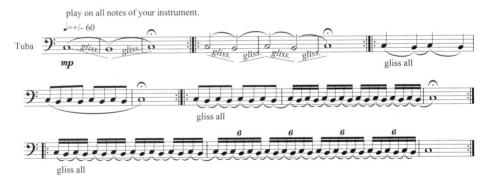

What goes *down* can also go *up*, so here's another great exercise, this time for an upwards-moving pitch vibrato. Take a very deep breath and start each note "saying" the syllables as written in the exercise. You'll notice that the back of your tongue moves higher as you change from AH to EE. Whilst this is happening, give more air (crescendo) and the pitch should rise. Don't use the valves, but do try to keep the tone beautiful. This is great for tuning those flat notes that occur on all tubas.

But Which Type, When?

With practice, you will have three choices of vibrato to deploy, depending on your ideas of how you want to sound in relation to the demands of the music you are performing. But which type of vibrato do you use at what time? Well, this is a matter of taste, of course, but if you listen to a 'cello playing, you will hear that mostly, the vibrato on low notes is slower and wider than on high notes. This has everything to do with the mechanics of the instrument, but sounds perfectly natural to our modern ears. High notes tend to get the "*fast and intense*" treatment, especially in louder dynamics. But wait a minute; wouldn't that also be good for showing climaxes in phrases? I think so! Let's look at this then as a general, rule of thumb. Low is slow; high is fast, remembering that rules are made to be broken under the right circumstances.

Here's an exercise that will help enhance your vibrato playing skills, whilst correcting your intonation and improving your tone at the same time.

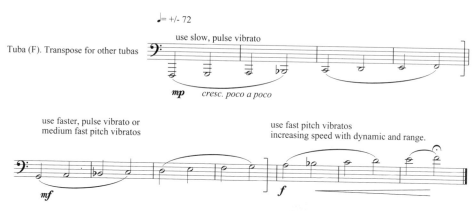

To hear a demonstration of all the above exercises, visit www.jamesgourlay.com

Don't forget that vibrato is most effective when it is used *sparingly* and when it sounds *natural*. Try to make it sound not too metered or predictable. Vibrato will enhance your sound, but it will not magically turn a poor tone into a great one. Don't forget to do your long tones! Listen also to those musicians who make vibrato part of their art, and you will be able to incorporate this valuable musical tool into your playing. ➤

Forza de Musica Marinara: A Nutritious Dish that, Carefully Prepared, Simmered, and Consumed Regularly, Will Promote Health and Build Strong 'Bones (Trumpets, Horns, and Tubas, Too)

Toby Hanks

INGREDIENTS:
A collection of exercises. Your instrument. A commitment to excellence.

SERVES:
All brass players.

Every student should devise an extensive collection of exercises to develop and maintain basic skills, i.e., tone quality, range, articulation, dynamics, flexibility, scales arpeggios, etc. This daily routine should take 30 to 45 minutes (one hour, tops) to complete. A developing student should be very consistent in completing the exercises five *or more* days per week.

In later life, the mature player doesn't need a daily dose, but these combined exercises will form a toolbox that can be used to trim up things that occasionally slip away a bit as we go through our lives as musicians.

What . . . ? Hard won skills slip away?! Say it ain't so!

Kids . . . trust me . . . you will understand some day.

There are many sources for these exercises . . . Remington, Stamp, Caruso, Clarke, Arban, Schloshberg, and more. Many unpublished teachers and players develop their own mix of these, plus their own things. The tried-and-true exercises are always great, but "it ain't rocket science," and these teacher/players often come up with a good mix for themselves and/or their students that is effective and can be trusted.

Warning 1
A daily routine is sometimes referred to as a "warm-up routine" . . . *not entirely so!* A **warm-up** is what we do to prepare ourselves to perform/rehearse/practice, which will vary depending on any number of things: such as what you have played lately, what you have *not* played lately, and what you have to do today. A **daily routine** is basic skills development. Included in your routine, over time, you will discover what you need to "warm up" for different situations. No need to do your entire routine backstage before rehearsals and concerts. To others it is boring, unnecessary, and annoying (no matter how musically you do it). Warm up as necessary . . . have some coffee . . . read the paper . . . talk to some friends . . . your routine is essentially for your own private practice.

Warning 2

Conscientious daily repetition of such a routine sometimes develops in some **DRDS** (Daily Routine Dependency Syndrome).

Primary Symptom

An inability to play comfortably at rehearsals or concerts unless this routine is completed. Be aware that *life will not always afford one this convenience.*

Antidote

1. Sprinkle the exercises in small doses throughout your practice day. (Similar benefits can be derived.)
2. Occasionally just pick up your instrument and play. Just keep your concepts strong. *Never mind how it feels.* Jake taught us that "it don't have to feel good to sound good." (God bless him.)

Warning 3

You need a balanced diet.

Playing exercises are not enough to develop the ability to interpret and communicate music to an audience, whether in solo, chamber, or orchestral settings. Musicality is the ability to communicate the character and emotional content of the music at hand to an audience. The various instrumental skills we learn are merely the tools we use. We must learn to use these tools effectively.

Spend a lot of time in this area . . . musical etudes, solos (concerti), and orchestral music should be studied extensively. *Interpret, interpret, interpret.* Be a storyteller! And anyway, these exercises should be executed as musically as possible. Why play *anything* that doesn't sound at least *somewhat* musical, if you can help it? Of course, you're not trying to tell your life story through exercises, and you may be striving to execute them in some specific way that may render them somewhat crude for a time, but always keep musical concepts strong, as you develop them. I hate "ugly," unless the music at hand requires it . . . and sometimes it does.

Since I brought up a "don't do" at work earlier, allow me to list a few other things to think about that apply to behavior, especially if you're a sub or new to a situation.

1. If you arrive and you don't know what part you are to play, sit at the last chair until informed otherwise. Or, don't sit down at all, until you are so informed.
2. Don't "prelude," defined by John Swallow as an attempt to show everyone the full range of your ability by playing solos or audition material for your upcoming audition. And especially, never practice parts that others will be playing. Just do your job well . . . no more, no less. You will thereby make others comfortable with you on the job personally and musically. You might even get asked back.
3. Don't bring drinks or food on to the stage or pit unless the regulars do.
4. Don't read newspapers onstage or pit unless the regulars do.
5. Dress appropriately, in a manner so as not to direct undue attention to your attire. You want to be noted for your professional excellence, not your style of dress. For social situations, do as you wish. On the job, dress professionally.

There are other do's and don'ts that could be listed, but just keep in mind that what we do is one of the highest forms of social cooperation in our culture. What other tasks require such training, discipline, cooperation, and pinpoint accuracy at any given *second!?* Therefore, we want to do everything we can to promote that cooperation in order to achieve the exhilarating product that attracted us to music in the first place, in such a way as not to spoil the fun. Always be thinking of what you can do to help. Playing your own part well is of course essential, but positive interactions with your teammates runs a close second in my experience; *and it isn't always easy.* ➤

Five Hors d'Oeuvres for Common Brass Player Ailments

Richard Hansen

Prevention of Red Rot

INGREDIENTS:
A little time
Clean water
A sink, tub, or shower
A snake

SERVES:
All brass players.

Many players are concerned with red rot usually found on the leadpipe or tuning crook (on trombones, the end bow of the slide). If left alone, leaks may eventually occur. Prevention/retardation is accomplished by removing the tuning crook and flushing the pipe and crook with water and the snake. Do at least once a week and you will be removing most of the acids that linger after playing the horn. Simple, effective, cheap.

Preventing Stuck Slides

INGREDIENTS:
Lubricant

SERVES:
All brass players.

Use a good lubricant such as any commercial brand , or—I have been flamed for this—STP motor oil treatment, or lanolin. I don't recommend Vaseline, as it seems to dry up quickly. Apply the lube and insert one tube at a time with a twisting motion. After this is done, move them often.

Getting a Stuck Valve to Move

INGREDIENTS:
A rawhide or plastic hammer (for rotary valves)
An extra piston valve (for piston valves)

SERVES:
All brass players.

For rotary valves, loosen the screw that holds the stop hub a turn or two. Tap the screw lightly with a rawhide or plastic hammer. The words "lightly" and "tap" should be remembered. Take the cap off and check the bearing plate. There should be no uneven gap between it and the casing. If there is, tap it back down so it rests evenly.

For piston valves, remove a piston and insert it from the bottom of the stuck piston. Tap *very* gently so you don't bend the good piston. Don't even think about using a drumstick or screwdriver.

Stuck Mouthpiece

INGREDIENTS:
A mouthpiece puller

SERVES:
All brass players.

Never use pliers; use a mouthpiece puller. These can be purchased from suppliers to the trade or from music stores. Some shops remove stuck mouthpieces free.

Cleaning Valves

INGREDIENTS:
A rough cloth
A Q-tip (or other cotton swab)
A cleaning rod
Detergent (optional)

SERVES:
All brass players.

Use rough cloth and scrub the valve and casing. Use a Q-tip for hard-to-reach areas. Use a cleaning rod with a cloth for the casings, and scrub well. For rotary casings, use whatever finger fits with the cloth wrapped around the tip. If your piston valves have a tobacco colored stain on them, let your favorite tech take it off. Clean your valves with detergent if you are changing from petroleum to synthetic oil. ➦

Ready...Set...Rehearse: A Basic Guide to Thinking Professionally in a Rehearsal Setting

Kevin Hayward

INGREDIENTS:
Positive mental attitude. Alert mind. Pencil(s).

SERVES:
Anyone seeking to improve their "rehearsal game."

Unless one is a soloist working exclusively with "tape," brass players have no choice but to work with other musicians in an ensemble setting. It goes without saying that all serious ensembles need to rehearse. Whether one is a church musician, student, serious hobbyist, or keenly seeking to join the professional ranks, everyone can benefit from a renewed focus on rehearsal participation.

The guiding thought when contemplating rehearsal participation is this: "What can I do to make a positive, significant, and satisfying contribution?"

Before You Take Your Seat:
I am told that in order to minimize potential problems during a flight, all pilots must follow a set routine (preflight checklist) before they prepare for take-off. While a rehearsal may not have the same potential for disaster as a flight, many problems can be avoided by having a basic rehearsal checklist. The following can be used as a basic template.

1. Ensure that you have everything you need to take with you: music/instrument stand, the music to be rehearsed, any requisite mutes, pencil(s), any emergency supplies (strings for rotors, lubricant for slides, valves, linkages, etc.)
2. Plan to arrive with time to spare. This shows respect for one's colleagues and allows for a relaxed start.

A Positive Start
Arguably the most important ingredient necessary for achieving optimal results in rehearsal is a positive mental attitude.

Being positive is the first step toward having a satisfying rehearsal experience. When one is enthusiastic, it is easier to contribute positive energy to what can otherwise be a negative experience. Being an encourager motivates colleagues and section mates, and can lead to invigorating and energizing results.

An Alert Mind

Being alert can make a big difference to the flow of rehearsal, in addition to what one gets out of it. The importance of one being appropriately analytical (impossible without an alert mind) can be illustrated by the constant consideration of the following:

Intonation: How is your intonation? Are you in tune? These questions are not just relevant to overall ensemble and section tuning, but need to be evaluated relative to the particular musical context on a moment-by-moment basis.

Articulation: Do your articulations match the intensity and shape of those of your section mates, or those playing similar lines or motifs?

Musicianship: What is your musical role? Foreground vs. background? Are you aware of the stylistic, historical demands of the music?

Rhythm: Is your use or absence of rhythmic emphasis correct, consistent, appropriate? Are you playing in time?

Ensemble: Are your choices for places to breathe complementary to your section in a relevant musical context? Do they match what others are doing around the ensemble (nonsection setting)? Is your use of tone color, vibrato, etc. appropriate, i.e., *complementary* to the ensemble?

Conductor . . . What Conductor?

Being attentive and alert to the rehearsal leader or conductor is especially important when one is seeking to be successful in the rehearsal hall. A pencil or two should always be at the ready to note any relevant comment the conductor/rehearsal leader may make.

Comments regarding nonintuitive conducting motions and ideas are of prime importance. Changes in tempo and complex patterns not indicated in one's part are critical items to be written down in a way that will draw your attention during performance. Atypical breathing spots that will assist in carrying a line etc. are also critical spots to be marked.

After the Rehearsal Has Ended:

At the conclusion of any rehearsal is when the real work begins.

1. Whatever has been learned about the future musical goals of the ensemble relevant to any piece of music should be reflected upon for areas needing further attention.
2. Areas of technical deficiency should be mercilessly attacked.
3. Listening to good recordings of the works to be performed may yield further musical insight. This is particularly helpful when preparing to perform very large works with minimal rehearsal.
4. Consulting with colleagues/section mates to work on difficult ensemble or *soli* passages is a sure way to ensure success at the next rehearsal/performance.

In Conclusion

This necessary part of the journey to musical achievement and performance can be a thrilling ride or a routine, necessary evil. The choice is yours!

The Four Ps

Lesley Howie

INGREDIENTS:
Preparation. Practice. Performance. Presentation.

SERVES:
All performers.

Preparation

In preparing for your performance, there are a number of things you should consider. In advance you should find out if there are any time limits. Be sure you know exactly how much time you are expected to be on stage for, and this will include all introductions and rests between pieces. Choice of repertoire is vital; be realistic and play to your strengths and not your weaknesses. Choose music that is within your capabilities and that highlights areas of your playing that you know you can do well. As you will be preparing for some time, it is also important that you enjoy the music that you have chosen. Make sure that you have a wide range of styles within the program so that your audience will hear a varied program.

As a soloist, it is also important to consider your accompaniment. Having a varied accompaniment will enhance your recital and keep it interesting. You may wish to utilize organ, string quartet, singers, or brass ensemble in addition to the standard piano accompaniment within your recital, even if this means you have to rearrange the music. In your preparation, you are not only learning the solo part; you should know the accompaniment equally well. Know how it sounds and mark in all possible cues on your solo part, as there is not always the opportunity for sufficient rehearsal time.

What are you going to wear? Is it practical and suitable? You want to look the part without being uncomfortable. If possible, it is a good idea to have a trial performance before the big day, wearing your outfit and in a similar environment to the one you will perform in.

Preparation is simply considering every possible aspect of the recital to ensure you have eliminated as many potential problems as you can.

Practice

Many players *think* they are practicing when really they are just playing. You could spend an hour "playing" your favorite pieces but what have you actually achieved or improved on by the end? When you have completed your warm-up, your practice time is there to improve on aspects of your playing. Have an organized practice regime, in which you spend allocated time on the areas that need improving. Practice related material to the repertoire you have chosen. For example, if a piece has lots of triple tonguing in it, spend time working on related exercises and studies.

Never leave anything for granted and mark as much direction as possible onto your music as you can, including: breath marks, accidentals, fingerings, additional dynamics, etc. You cannot rely on yourself to remember everything in a stressful situation.

Don't leave it too late. Leave yourself plenty of time in advance to practice and learn the repertoire. Listen to recordings of other performers playing the music you have chosen and playing music by the same composer or in a similar style. You don't want to copy another performer, but getting a more in-depth knowledge of the music can only enhance your own performance. Try recording yourself, then listen and analyze the playing. It can be an interesting exercise. As a listener, you may pick up on things that you didn't realize you were doing as a performer.

Again, be realistic. If something is only occasionally right during your practice, then the chances are it won't be right on stage, either.

Your practice should take your playing to a standard where you have a consistent performance of your program. At this point, you should be running your recital program on a daily basis. Build up strength and stamina over a period of time before the recital. If you know you can play your program twice in one day, then you should be confident to know that you will easily get through it once on the recital day.

Performance

You have done the practice and the preparation, and finally the recital day arrives. At this point you should feel confident that you are fully prepared. However, even if the work in the practice room has been good, this does not automatically mean the performance will be. Performance means that you must deliver as much as you can in a once-off situation.

Prepare yourself for things that could go wrong and accept them. Don't change anything that you have practiced at the last minute; the chance of your risk-taking paying off is slim. Hence the reason for all your hard work in preparing and practice: to eliminate as many potential problems as possible. Don't create more! Concentrate throughout the performance and don't let any slips affect you. Forget any slips immediately and worry about them afterwards. Smile and carry on, continuing to concentrate on the present moment, not two bars ago where you made a mistake.

Presentation

Presentation is the art of performance. Performance is like an act and begins from the second you walk on stage. Remember that audiences can hear and see! Smile as you walk on, keeping your head high and looking at the audience—never look at the floor! It is your job as a performer to please the audience and get them on your side. Maintain good eye contact and smile during any rests. To do this, the audience needs to see you, so carefully position your music stand (if you use one). Know how you are going to hold your instrument and stand comfortably in rests or whilst speaking to the audience. If you shuffle about or look uneasy the audience *will* notice. Be comfortable with the bow and accepting the audience applause. You have worked hard and deserve it, so enjoy the moment. However, don't forget to acknowledge your accompanist. Stand him/her up and take a bow together.

Most importantly, when you are prepared and practiced, you should enjoy your performance! ➤●

The Winning Difference: Making an Audition Count

Gregory Hustis

Hundreds of performance majors graduate every year from colleges and conservatories poised to enter the highly competitive world of orchestral auditions. There are too many qualified people for only a handful of available positions. What recipe for success will set you apart from the pack? Aside from a regimen of quality practicing, how else can you train mentally and physically in order to make the most of your audition efforts? How can you prepare yourself so that you will perform at your highest level at each audition? Below is a recipe for audition success—one that will prepare you to play your very best.

INGREDIENTS:
Your instrument
A metronome and tuner
A good recording device (a MiniDisc recorder is probably best)
Complete parts of the pieces you're preparing
A CD player and CDs of the excerpts to be played at the audition
A notebook or journal
Reading materials
A few colleagues

SERVES:
Anyone wishing to improve his/her audition skills.

Before taking an audition, make sure that your instrument and all of your equipment are in excellent working order. It's amazing how unmanageable even the smallest problem can become in an audition situation.

Be sure to use a tuner and metronome in all stages of audition preparation. Don't become totally dependent on such tools, but use them regularly to check rhythm, tempos, intonation, and intervals. Anyone who has been on the listening side of the audition screen can tell you that the main reason for initial dismissal is poor rhythm.

It is always wise, whenever possible, to have a complete part of each work you will be playing at an audition, even if you are asked to play only a few bars from that work. Excerpt books are acceptable in some cases, but only if you don't have the real part. Technically, a committee could ask you to play anything, not just those few bars on the list. Most parts can be obtained through Kalmus. Those excerpts not available to purchase are usually provided by the orchestra asking for them.

A particularly important ingredient in this audition preparation recipe is a good recording device. Although you may not be able to make reliable assessments of your tone with a recorder, it is amazing what other things you can learn. Recordings do not lie. Rhythmic inconsistencies and a lack of articulation clarity that may never have been apparent to you while practicing will glare out unmercifully on a recorded playback. Intonation issues will be painfully obvious. People usually find that their dynamic range and musical expressiveness are much more limited than they thought. Record yourself several times a week, and start far in advance of the audition so that positive changes can be incorporated into your playing.

Next in the list of ingredients: Several recordings of different orchestras performing all the works on your audition list. Listen to what the rest of the orchestra is doing during your audition excerpt. As you perform each excerpt, hear the accompanying parts in your mind. This will help improve rhythmic accuracy, keep proper dynamics, and, in general, raise musical awareness. Does the style you're playing truly fit the music? How does a player inject his/her personal style into each excerpt, yet still remain true to what the composer has written? Here is where you have a real opportunity to set yourself apart from the other people auditioning for the job. Many players are technically capable and consistent, but because there is very little room for rhythmic and technical interpretation in an excerpt, musical interpretation is especially important. You should know precisely what you want to express with each excerpt. Recordings are a good place to start to compile musical ideas. Begin by listening to what others have done, and then build your own ideas from there. No one wins an important audition without displaying excellent musicianship, which comes from creative artistry and being musically well schooled.

Another main ingredient to the recipe is a practice journal. This is a great way to stay organized and to become more consistent. Write down long- and short-term goals, and keep a daily log of your progress in all areas. It's amazing how efficient practice time can become through keeping a practice journal.

What follows are few recommendations that can be thought of as optional special spices to add to your recipe. Run your audition list in more than one practice space. You don't want to get too used to playing in one place only; acoustical differences can be disrupting. Practice in big rooms or halls, but also in smaller spaces. Play the excerpts in a different order every day. For example, put the excerpts in the most difficult order you can think of—this may be how you'll have to play them in the audition!

Write down a few adjectives at the top of each excerpt. Excerpts from *Til Eulenspiegel* and Tchaikovsky *Symphony No. 5* may be back to back in the audition—that's a lot of different emotional ground to cover in a short period of time. A few descriptive words can pull you into the right frame of mind very quickly. Consistency is the name of the game. Make up drills during your practice sessions in order to increase consistency. Devote time to playing an excerpt ten times in a row *perfectly*. You'll be amazed by how much you will learn and accomplish.

Many books have been written to help musicians and athletes perform (audition!) at their highest level. These books are especially valuable to those players who are susceptible to performance jitters. A few examples of the best of these books are *Zen in the Art of Archery* by Eugen Herrigel, *Performance Stress* by Don Greene, and a particular favorite of mine, *The New Toughness Training for Sports* by James E. Loehr.

After putting together all the ingredients, try your completed recipe out on a few colleagues by playing the audition list for them. This will be a chance to receive some new ideas and to simulate the stress of a real audition. Play both for people who play your instrument and for those who do not. A clarinetist will be far less forgiving of a horn player's cracked notes than another horn player will be! You may even decide to set up a realistic mock audition. Some people have gone so far as to put up a screen to play behind so that they are mentally prepared for every last detail of what they will encounter.

Playing auditions well is an art in itself. This recipe will help you to leave nothing to chance. You will sharpen your skills and be confident in knowing you did everything possible to be well prepared. Those who win jobs are those who are both technically secure and musically compelling.

Good luck.

Making Arban's a Supplement to Your Daily Routine

Alex Iles

Arban's *Complete Method* may be the most common method book among brass players all over the world. Nearly every brass player has encountered this book at some point in his/her musical development.

On first sight, many players can become confused or frustrated by the scope of the material in this book. Should you go through the book page by page? Should you skip around a little? Should you make up/improvise the material by ear instead of reading it out of a book? I would like offer a way to do all three of these things using the material presented in this classic book for brass playing.

INGREDIENTS:

Your instrument. *Arban's Famous Method for Trombone*, edited by Randall Mantia. Encore Publishing's *Arban's Complete Method for Trombone and Euphonium*, edited by Joseph Alessi and Dr. Brian Bowman.

SERVES:

Trombone and euphonium players.

In the outline below, I list twelve of the most important topics I like to address on a regular basis as part of my daily low brass playing routine and what exercises from Arban's I might use as I address that topic. What I actually play on any given practice session might be drawn from a variety of books, lesson notes, improvised exercises, or music I am preparing for upcoming performances.

After a brief warm-up, and depending on how much time I have that day, I will focus on any one of the following topics for 5, 10, or maybe 20 minutes, then move on to another, rest a little, then perhaps come back to an earlier topic for more focused or specific work.

There are many other topics I like to cover in my daily practice—breathing, improvisational ideas, songs by ear, range expansion, extended techniques, etc.— but below are twelve of the topics I go to Arban's for the most.

The page numbers below refer to the Randall/Mantia version of *Arban's Famous Method for Trombone*. The page numbers in brackets refer to the Alessi/Bowman edition of Arban's, referred to as "A/B".

1. **Mouthpiece/Buzzing**

   p. 19 [A/B p. 15] #9 [on mouthpiece, then on horn]

2. **Sound**

   p. 108 [A/B p. 119] #44–47 in a singing, *bel canto* style. More of this material appears in the Alessi/Bowman version—great for sight-singing/playing.

3. **Slower Slurs and Intervals**

   p. 45 [A/B p. 44] #3–11, p. 47 [A/B p. 47] #16 and 17
   p. 135 [A/B p. 147] #8–12

4. **Slow Articulated Playing**

   p. 45 [A/B p. 43] #1 and 2

   p. 93 [A/B p. 101] #1 (eighth note = 60 or slower)

5. **Faster Slurs/Trills**

   p. 48 [A/B p. 48] #18–26

6. **Faster Articulated Playing . . . the subject I draw out of Arban's most**

   p. 53 [A/B p. 54] #31–60
   p. 93 [A/B p. 101] #1–23
   p.110 [A/B p. 121] #48–54, no grace notes
   p.136 [A/B p. 148] #13–47, triplets and sixteenths

7. **Slow Scales**

   p. 63–90 [A/B p. 64–86]. Try starting with one or two keys/day every week for a few months . . . eighth note = 50!

8. **Faster Scales**

   p. 24 [A/B p. 22] #28–45
   p. 28 [A/B p. 27] #47–50
   p. 63 [A/B p. 65] #1–16 are different patterns in B♭; the remaining keys have six patterns each. Take one key through all six of these patterns in a practice session then derive your own patterns in that key. Unfortunately, Arban's only goes through the flat keys. Do the sharp keys too!
   p. 80–90 [A/B p. 88–99] #1–30. I might read an exercise then repeat it by ear starting on a different note.

9. **Faster/Wider Intervals**

   p. 126–127 [A/B p. 139–140] . . . play p. 127 [A/B p. 140], top to bottom (no repeats), *mf*, with a good solid *tenuto* attack, then shift over to p. 128 [A/B p. 139] and read it from the bottom up. Rest briefly every couple of lines. Over time, you will be able both pages without needing to rest as much. Work this up from about quarter note = 72 if you are an intermediate player, and work it up day by day, week by week, month by month to 160 or more. Strive for a resonant sound at all times through all registers.

10. **Multiple Tonguing**

    p. 162 [A/B p. 175] #1–14, triple-tongued triplet patterns on a single note. Don't rush your way through these. Play them very *slowly* (quarter note = 60–72 at first). Experiment with articulating TTK, TKT, TTT, TKK, and KKK so that the Ts and Ks become equally clear and practically interchangeable.
    p. 167 [A/B p. 179] #16–46. Triple-tongue across one, then two intervals.

p. 175 [A/B p. 187] #47–76. Triple-tongue on scales and intervals. You can go back to the exercises used in #6 above for more triple-tongue practice, too. The double-tongue section then moves through the process a little quicker. (Maybe Arban figured that if you made it this far with triple tonguing, you should pick up double tonguing pretty quickly.) In this section, there are some nice mixed articulation (double tongue/slurred) exercises to expand your faster articulation repertoire. Crispness, clarity, great time, and great sound should be a higher priority than speed.

11. **Rhythmic Accuracy/Style**

p. 30 [A/B p. 29] #1–18. Strive for clear consistent time on these. Check yourself against a metronome occasionally. Slide and tongue work together!

p. 35 [A/B p. 35] #19–37. This is in my "top 5" of single tongue exercises! Start very slowly. Make each of these exercises lock in rhythmically. Time permitting, I will often do three to four of these a day. Tongue speed and sense of time are closely related. Strive first for efficiency, good time, and clarity. Eventually, speed will come.

12. **Arpeggios**

p. 60 [A/B p. 62] #68–69. Major chords, taken through various inversions. On #69, all the keys are right there in front of you! No excuses!

p. 151 [A/B p. 160] Major: #48, 50, and 52; Minor: #49 and 51; Dominant 7: #53; Diminished 7: #55. Again, all keys are right there! Get to work, even if you start *really* slow! I like to do three to four keys at a practice session. Let's them soak in. Strive to be comfortable doing these by ear. Close your eyes and *blow!*

This leaves the famous *Characteristic Studies* and the *Airs and Variations.* As you work through the material above, you will be developing the necessary tools to jump into these technically challenging pieces. You may also try inserting certain phrases from these etudes and adding them to any of the categories above.

Be imaginative and creative, especially when you work through "exercises." Focusing on fundamentals does not have to lead to mechanical playing. Let the tools you develop become transparent and instinctual. That way, your attention ultimately leads back to just making beautiful music.

Good luck! ➤

The Brass Player's Guide to the Galaxies: The Art of Arriving Refreshed and Ready to Play Your Best

Ingrid Jensen

After many years of road life and endless encounters with the inevitable "out of control" elements, I have finally come up with a fairly reliable travel method. In the same way that I have experimented with techniques from different trumpet teachers, I have followed suit by trying out advice that friends and various sources have imparted on me in the arena of travel.

Be it train, plane, bus, or boat, there is one consistent element that allows me to play my best when I get to the gig: sleep. Without sleep, things start going wrong. From dropped mouthpieces to physical injuries to lost belongings, the cycle of mistakes gets rolling and things go awry. No matter how much espresso or vitamins are ingested, the body just gets fed up and says "no" to the demands we put on it. It's really true that we get paid to get to the gig, not to play—that's the easy part!

Not to take away from the euphoric playing space that I often enjoy playing from when arriving exhausted or jet-lagged—but again, the sleep-deprived player can make mistakes they never made before when rest has been denied.

My travel recipe takes a bit of preparation time and can be modified according to each individual's budget. Drawing on the ingredients from either the basic or the advanced recipe will make for a refreshed and healthy state of arrival.

You must also be willing to accept that you may appear a bit funny looking to friends and fellow travelers, so it is best to remember that they are in the same potentially sleepless situation as you. Regardless of the length of the trip you are taking, always be prepared to crash out safely. Unless you are on a prop plane, you will experience G-force pressure on take-off, which is the time when you are most likely to fall asleep. It can also be the time when you fall asleep in a nasty position, waking up with a stiff neck and a sore back. Following the recipe below can help you to avoid injuries and arrive refreshed and ready to play your best.

BASIC INGREDIENTS (FOR ON THE PLANE AND IN THE AIRPORT):
Earplugs
Neck pillow
Seat pillow
Eye mask
Water
Chewable vitamin C
Dr. Bach Rescue Remedy™ (also available in an alcohol-free base)
Blanket or jacket long enough to cover your legs

Teas (chamomile and/or Sleepy Time)
Air purifier
Extras: Books, Travel Scrabble, music (iRiver), computer, DVDs, *Silent Brass* mute, Gripmaster™–medium strength, and Bose headphones.

SERVES:
All brass players and beyond.

Preparation
Pack sleeping gear in your carry-on that you will place under your seat or have closest to you. Drink plenty of liquids and eat a fairly large meal about an hour before take-off.

Directions
Insert earplugs, sit on seat pillow, inflate neck pillow, drink some water, chew on a vitamin C (every three hours or so), and strap on your air purifier (around your neck).

If you can't sleep, take some Dr. Bach drops and drink a cup of tea.

If you are exhausted, sleep! If flying into another time zone, try to set your inner clock to hook up with that zone and stay awake until you reach a time that will make it easier to adjust when you arrive. Then sleep.

Avoid eating if you can, and take a break from caffeine at all costs. I often take juice boxes with me that curb my appetite and help me through the hunger pains. It's a night-and-day difference on the jet lag when eating is kept to a minimum or avoided completely. *Try it!*

Benefits
You will arrive rested, fairly hydrated, and injury- and disease-free.

Thoughts from the Author
The bonus of this travel approach is that not only do you get that hard-to-obtain sleep, but you can avoid catching the many bugs that are out there and actually boost your immune system in the process.

As well, if you remember to bring all of the above ingredients, you can actually get to the music and practice when flights are delayed, or when you have scored you own row on the plane, or are just sitting on a bus or a train, daydreaming the day away while fingering through the music (Gripmaster™) you are off to play.

Where to Find the Supplies
Bach drops can be found at any health food store, seat and neck pillows at travel stores and outdoor outfitting stores, Brookstone® air purifier online or at your local Brookstone® store. The best earplugs I seem to find at the local pharmacy.

Happy trails! ➤●

Clearing the Air—Do You Really Need to Learn How to Breathe?

Dave Kirk

Tubists are often considered experts on matters respiratory, and with some justification. Any accomplished player you've enjoyed hearing has likely given some thought to how they produce the air, resulting in beautiful sound, enhanced flexibility, and crisp articulation.

In lessons I teach, time is spent addressing breathing, but it's often a process of simplifying concepts. I've discovered there is a great deal of information creating barriers to progress.

Stated simplistically, if you're reading this article, you've done an outstanding job of breathing for *[insert your age here]* years, right up to this moment. Congratulations, you already know how to breathe! For wind players, our obvious issue is obtaining and utilizing a large quantity of air.

The problems I see are in deviations away from the natural process, including but not limited to:

- over-analyzed vowel-inflected inhalation
- reliance on resetting the embouchure
- overemphasis on the role of the mouth in inhalation
- excessive speed and/or tension in inhalation (and resulting exhalation)

I will argue each of these points, and offer some simple exercises to emphasize a return to the natural path.

INGREDIENTS:
A desire to simplify your breathing

A tonal concept of beautiful sound, flexibility, and crisp articulation

SERVES:
All breathing musicians.

Breathing vowels. Many players are taught to think of the letter "O" during inhalation. I believe the "ah" sound to be more natural. To illustrate, speak the words "Tom" and "Toe," holding out the final vowel sound of each word. What feels more relaxed in the oral cavity and throat? To achieve greater resonance, constrict less.

Resetting. Purposefully or not, many players reset the position of the mouthpiece each time a breath is taken. I liken this to a violinist lifting the bow completely off the instrument between each phrase, something you'll never see at a concert where there's paid admission. Adequate air may be taken through the sides of the mouth, or by backing away slightly from the instrument at the moment of refilling. It is most important to maintain the embouchure, as we seek to develop the strength and flexibility of a single point of placement. As we breathe, we strive to maintain the position of tone quality.

Mouth breathing. This is essential in wind performance. You can't beat it for quantity! That said, consider for a moment that the majority of breathing we do everyday is with the nose. The nose breath is comparatively more relaxed and smoother. I encourage players to work towards incorporating *both* nose and mouth for inhalation. For some this is a novel idea. Check yourself the next time you do some highly aerobic activity. You'll see how efficiently mouth and nose work in tandem when the body demands maximum airflow. When playing, we seek to have the gentle, relaxed quality of the nasal breath instruct the complete process.

"Turbo-breathing." The breathing we do when making music should be an uncomplicated extension of what we already do. Methods or approaches taking a player away from this basic concept are counterproductive. Recognizing the necessity for quick breaths within musical phrases, those breaths should be trained within the principles previously stated.

To illustrate this point, try a simple exercise I call "The Five Breaths," first done *without your instrument.*

Take a breath and make the exhalation of . . .

1. A *pianissimo* long note (25 percent of capacity)
2. The same note at *mezzo piano* (40 percent)
3. A *mezzo forte* well-supported sound (65 percent)
4. A *forte* with great projection (80 percent)
5. A *fortissimo*, noble tone (95 percent)

Each successive breath/exhalation is built upon the last. Your process remains the same; the volume and projection increases. Now try it on your instrument and listen to your sound fill a room (at every dynamic).

Exhalation

A subject often overlooked in discussion of respiration is **exhalation**. If students struggle with taking a full and relaxed breath, I encourage them to first blow all the air out of their lungs. By creating a need, a deep inhalation always follows, and the basics of good playing have once again found their foundation.

I also encourage players, as they prepare to make entrances, to make a habit of exhaling in time with the established pulse of the music, then bringing the breath back a beat before the entrance. By using this method of purposeful deprivation to create natural desire, we reinforce a habit of good musicianship.

Exhalation feeds tone. Rarely will compliments be given for your method of breathing, but the tone, naturally supported, is always a source of wonder for audiences. ➤

Let Go and Share the Music: How to Practice Making Music (Not Just Creating Perfection)

Craig Knox

INGREDIENTS:
An impending performance or audition. Adequate preparation time. A recording device (optional).

SERVES:
Any musician who wants to "get past the notes."

Be Clear in Your Purpose

When preparing a piece of music for performance, it is easy to be consumed with producing a perfectly executed rendition of the work. This can be particularly true when preparing excerpts for an audition, since the "pieces" are disconnected from their true musical context and are often extremely technically challenging, to boot. If you find yourself going down this path, it is worthwhile to remind yourself what your purpose is as a musician. Remember that people do not go to a concert to witness the creation of perfection; they go to be moved. Your job is to express the joy, the excitement, the beauty of the music, and share it with the audience. If you adopt a protective stance in which your top priority is the preservation and re-creation of your "perfect" rendition, the result is likely to come across as stiff and overly engineered. No matter how clean and accurate your playing is, it is not likely to grab the listener unless you are willing to really take chances, even at the risk of imperfection.

While all of this may seem obvious when contemplating a recital performance, it may not seem as relevant to auditions. Auditions, after all, are competitions in which your playing is meticulously scrutinized and judged. However, audition panels are made up of actual people who are subject to the same influences as any other audience. While an audition committee will certainly be listening for details along the way, they will always be drawn to a player who plays with ease, fearlessness, and inspired musicianship. Certainly, to be successful in an audition, you must be able to execute the excerpts, but the sooner you think of an audition committee as an audience with which to connect, the better.

Practice What You Preach

Taking chances and prioritizing communication with your audience may sound like a great idea, but the next step is to have a practice strategy that develops that ability. If you want to develop your high register, you must practice the high register; if you want to develop a great *legato*, you must practice *legato*. If you want to develop the ability to get down to sharing your music, you must practice just that.

A typical practice session may include a lot of earnest hard work on a piece of music, followed by one or two run-throughs (perhaps with interruptions for corrections) to tie it all together. However, this approach has some unintended consequences. By the time you get around to running the complete piece of music (which is what you are preparing to do after all, right?), your head is filled with all sorts of details and objectives that you have identified and worked on during your session. It will be very difficult at this point to put the minutiae aside and focus on the "big picture" during a run-through. Even more importantly, your run-through has now become a "test" to see how many of the details you worked so hard on you will now be able to duplicate . . . and that can lead to distracted and tentative playing. And, if you fail to ace all the spots you have worked on, you end up psychologically reinforcing the notion that, despite a lot of hard work, you still can't play this piece and you'll never be able to.

Consider this alternative. (This is for a piece you have already essentially learned and are now polishing for performance.):

1. Give some careful thought to establishing the overall character of the piece. What style and mood are you trying to convey to the listener? What excites or touches you about this music that you want to share with your audience? Formulate a picture or a scene in your mind, or an adjective or phrase that captures the spirit of the piece. Also be as clear in your mind as you can on the details of tempo, dynamics, articulation, phrasing, etc.

2. Play through the piece *in its entirety*, as a committed performance, focusing especially on bringing out the character of the music that you established in step 1. Go for it, play with abandon, have fun, and see what happens. Record the run-through if you wish. But, *do not stop for any reason*. Do not stop and start over because you are unsatisfied with how it is going. Do not stop to fix something or try something again. Playing the piece all the way through without interruptions has at least two benefits: first, because you have committed to play without stopping to fix things that go wrong, your concentration will tend to improve noticeably, in an effort to get it right the *first* time. Second, you will gain experience playing the piece the way you will ultimately perform it in concert. Playing through without stopping may be very difficult at first. But the more you do it, the easier it will become, as your concentration improves and you have fewer and fewer reasons to want to stop!

3. *Now* fix the things you are not satisfied with. Consult your memory of the run-through or the recording you made, and identify the spots that need attention. Spend this important time using your metronome, tuner, and other practice methods (this is a subject for another chapter!) to really work the details and address the problems as completely as you can.

4. *Leave it.* This step may be as hard for you as step 2. You may feel compelled at this point to run it through again (and again!) to see if you can do it better. But have *trust* in yourself that the progress you made in step 3 will stay with you and still be there when you run the piece in tomorrow's practice session. Having trust in oneself is perhaps the most important trait for a musician and, when developed, allows you to really focus on the music when performing.

Performing for People

Performing for others is the best way to practice performing music. When preparing for a performance, find people to play for ahead of time, whether they are family members, classmates, friends, teachers, or colleagues. Take it a step further, and seek out performance opportunities wherever you can find them. Play at a school, nursing home, hospital, church, or community center. Performing in any of these settings will help you develop the confidence to play your best in other situations, such as a recital, jury, competition, or audition. Really, though, these sorts of "practice concerts" are more than a means to an end. Performing for other people—in any situation—is what it's all about. Ideally you will realize that as a musician, your job is always the same: to share your most committed musical performance with your audience, no matter who they may be. ➡●

Interpreting Composers' Markings: Relative or Absolute

Mark H. Lawrence

As one who has been performing as soloist, chamber musician, and orchestral musician for almost fifty years, I have always been fascinated by the way performers and conductors interpret composers' markings and instructions to the performer. There are definitely two types of performers: those who take markings literally and those who don't. It's my strong belief that a composers markings are to be taken very loosely and only as guidelines to performance.

INGREDIENTS:
Dynamics. Tempo and style markings. Articulation markings.

SERVES:
Students, orchestral musicians, chamber musicians, soloists, jazz musicians, and band musicians.

Ingredient 1: Dynamics

One of the most important aspects of performance, especially ensemble performance, is the interpretation of dynamics written in the music. As ensemble performers, we play music from many different periods and by composers of many different nationalities and backgrounds. We should take this into consideration when we choose how to interpret dynamic markings. I feel it is a big mistake to be literal when considering what is on the printed page. I know of performers to whom a *forte* is a *forte*, no matter what the circumstances or the composer or the period in which the piece was written. I feel this does a disservice to the music and to your colleagues.

The two most important attributes to have in interpreting dynamics are your intuitive musical sense and your ear. When deciding how loud or soft to play in any given situation, I consider the following, not necessarily in order of importance:

- Who is the composer? Some composers, such as Tchaikovsky and Bruckner, write extremes of dynamics that need to be sometimes taken with a grain of salt.
- When was the piece written? Pieces written in the eighteenth and nineteenth centuries were dealing with a much different sounding ensemble, and brass instruments with much less dynamic possibilities. Their *fortissimos* for instance would be much different then our modern *fortissimos*.
- How big is the ensemble? I would play a much different dynamic in a 100-piece orchestra than I would in a 50-piece chamber orchestra, or a brass quintet.

- What type of space am I playing in? Halls that seat upwards of three thousand people require a different type of playing than ones that seat 1,500.
- What does the conductor like, if there is one? Do they like to hear a lot of brass or not?
- Do I have the melody or a supporting line? A melody line marked *mp* might need to be played *forte* in some cases to be heard, whereas a supporting line marked *forte* might need to be played *piano*.
- Do I need to blend or cut through the group? Band players in a group of ten trombones, for instance, need to play in a different way than an orchestral section of three.

Ingredient 2: Tempo and Style Markings

Tempo and style marking interpretation apply more to soloists and chamber musicians. In large ensembles, these markings are usually determined by the conductor. I view tempo and style markings in the same way as dynamics. Tempo and style, along with dynamics, are some of the most important tools musicians have in expressing themselves on their instruments. Once again, a composer's markings should be used as a guide to a performer's interpretation of the music. One should not discount what is in the performer's heart and soul when playing a piece of music. After all, that is what moves an audience most.

When learning a piece, I first play it through using the composer's markings as my guide. As I get to know a piece better, I put more and more of my own style and interpretation into the performance. This applies to tempos as well. I will start with a composer's marking and may change it based on my own needs as a performer. If we didn't do this, we would lose individuality as performers. I like listening to several different performers play the same piece and all sound different. A chamber music group can discuss these things as a group, and come to a mutually agreeable decision. All the groups I have been a member of have done this, and quite often the finished product is quite different from when the piece was first played. It can even vary from performance to performance, and this, I think, is a good thing.

Ingredient 3: Articulation Markings

Articulation markings apply mainly to different types of accents, *tenuto*, *legato*, *staccato*, and the profile of a note in any given situation. Here again, the composers markings should not be taken literally. There are several different types of accents, which can be very confusing to the performer, especially because not every composer uses them in the same way. Bruckner, for instance, sometimes writes accents on just about every note that is not *legato*. Does that mean you play every note with an accent? Not necessarily. You take into consideration that he was an organist and notated markings as an organist. When that translates to modern brass instruments, it should not be interpreted literally.

Similarly, when I am playing Brahms, the type of *staccato* I play will be drastically different than when I play Stravinsky. Brahms' *staccato* is more full-bodied and warm, while Stravinsky's is very dry and crisp. Sometimes a *legato* phrase might need to be tongued more firmly to not sound muddy from the audience. Likewise, an accent sometimes means you should decay on the note after the accent, and sometimes it means you should not. Once again, performers should use musical intelligence, and add that to the composer's intentions by listening very closely to what is going on in around them instead of blindly following the markings on the page.

To sum this all up, the underlying purpose of this article is to get musicians (young and old) to take more personal responsibility for their performance by listening closely to what's going on around them while performing, and using their musical intelligence to interpret a composer's intentions rather than by using an inflexible and literal interpretation, which requires no thought. If we all strive to do this, our performances will all benefit. ➤

Pitch and Rhythm Brew

John Marcellus

INGREDIENTS:
1 brain
2 critical ears
1 well-balanced body with healthy lungs
1 recording device (MiniDisc, DAT, computer [CD R+W or DVD R+W], video camera, CD, cassette or tape recorder with two speeds
1 tuning device
1 metronome
1 decibel meter (available at Radio Shack)
Optional: 1 *SmartMusic®* Studio by MakeMusic (which includes a metronome and tuner)

ADD:
Unlimited use of practice; mix well and serve.

SERVES:
Music and the multitudes (our listeners).

Very few instrumentalists seem to get past the first round of solo auditions in this age, mainly because of the basics of pitch, rhythm, and quality of sound. These musical necessities must be internalized in the subconscious mind without any external help from a performing organization, because they aren't present for your solo audition! This recipe is for brewing your pitch and rhythm. Sound quality is another recipe unto itself.

Intonation is affected by the natural overtones of your instrument and you must know which partials of the overtones that have a tendency to be sharp or flat. Check out your tendencies with the use of a tuning device in open or 1st position at three different dynamic levels of *pp, mf,* and *ff,* and chart them on a graph. As you descend chromatically on every valve combination or slide position, it is very revealing to see the results of the various dynamics on the tuner. Chart these also.

Place a decibel meter on a music stand in front of you with the silver-tip microphone pointed up toward the ceiling set on 110 dB. (dB ratings are always relative and not exactly rocket science with this method.) The dynamic marking *ff,* in this setting, should register close to 110 dB, which is "0" in the center of the meter.

Set the meter on 100 dB, and *mf* should register around 100 dB, which is in the center of the meter. The dynamic marking *pp,* at this 100 dB setting, should register around 94 dB or less. (This will vary, depending on the height of the music stand and the size of the room you are in.) When the needle goes into the red area at *ff*, notice the quality of sound you produce. It might be too raucous and not centered at higher levels above 116 dB. Notice as you ascend into the high register the difference in volume on the decibel meter, particularly at the softer levels. High notes are naturally louder than the low notes.

Too much tension in the body while holding the instrument and higher dynamics account for bad intonation in loud passages, because they are more difficult to control with the embouchure and air supply. Relaxation at all dynamics can't be stressed enough. Strength in the lip muscles and abdominal support must be gradually built up to help control the pitch in louder dynamics. (Endurance must also be built up; this calls for another recipe.)

Utilization of a tempered scale is a necessity to perform your solo audition. You must realize that the tuning you use in the ensemble is a different system (just intonation). Melodies, arpeggios, or scales with a "tempered" approach can be practiced by performing in unison with the keyboard (requires a performer) or set the *SmartMusic®* system to playback the melody in unison as you perform. Deficiencies in tempered pitch will be more noticeable with this approach at various dynamics. There is no substitute for practice.

Another variation in your practice is to enter your excerpts on a music notation program and play in unison with them. You can practice this *ad infinitum* and still not play a tempered melody in tune by yourself. Record your excerpts without the aid of the "helper" and listen to them as you play it back. Another variation for checking pitch can be performing your excerpt on a keyboard in unison with the playback. You can also perform on playback very softly on your instrument to hear discrepancies. Other practice aids include singing through a passage with the voice, or buzzing it on your mouthpiece. This can only enhance your internalization of the pitches in your mind's ear. The ultimate in better pitch control is to develop an instantaneous feedback of pitch perception with your ears while you are actually performing. Use the acoustics of a large hall to your advantage.

Rhythm or pulse without an ensemble to maintain the beat can also become a problem in the solo audition. Steady rhythm is a "feeling" to be developed and internalized. Organize your music so that the downbeat is primary and other beats in the measure are secondary to this pulse. Notice that when a music line ascends, the rhythm may pull back in tempo; when the music line descends, the rhythm may have a tendency to rush. The subdivision of the basic beat to the smaller beat (i.e., in 4/4, subdividing the beat into eighth notes) is a most important factor in "feeling" and imagining the beat as you play. Perform with the use of subdivision without affecting the melody or overemphasizing the pulse in the tone. A note of longer duration or a tied note in the music is also where we have a tendency to not keep track of the beat. The metronome is a big help to realize that a pulse is not steady but you must "lead" the metronome, not just follow it.

The breath is one of the biggest culprits that can affect your rhythm. The breath between phrases must become your metronome when you perform solo. The music dictates how fast or slow the rhythmic inhalation needs to be. Practice with different rhythmical inhalations, i.e., duple breath, triplet breath. You will notice that the quick breath after the subdivision of a note will help a phrase to not have too many "holes" or gaps in your sound.

Dynamics also affect rhythm in softer passages, which sometimes speed up, while louder dynamics will have a tendency to slow the beat down. Various registers present other problems with rhythm and less tension and more relaxation in the body will always help your performance. *Less is more.*

The same practice techniques in studying intonation are also applicable to rhythm. To check your rhythm on playback: record at the fast speed and playback at the slower speed, or play along with your recording at a softer dynamic. Placing a microphone at the other end of the room next to a metronome set at your tempo while recording is very revealing when played back!

Mix these well, and remember that time and tide wait for no man. ➤●

Old Music on New Horns

Raymond Mase

Whether it's the standard Robert King editions of Holborne or Gabrieli, or something more exotic with piccolo trumpets and nifty ornamentation, Renaissance music has a place in every brass quintet's library. The music works for every occasion from formal chamber music recitals to street-corner gigs. Here's a recipe to put together early music editions that are fun to play, interesting to listen to, and also capture a more authentic Renaissance flavor.

INGREDIENTS:
A willing and able brass quintet
Some music from around 1600, preferably unedited
A little imagination

SERVES:
All kinds of brass quintet performance.

Authentic Performance Practice?
Every responsible performer has to address the question of how to perform music written in another era. The two opposing views are to either attempt to perfectly recreate the music in the way we believe it sounded when it was written, or to simply play it in any way that suits us today and not worry about the past. But does either plan really work for brass quintet playing of early music? Well, we could try to go the authentic route, but let's face it, trying to make modern brass sound like cornets and sackbuts just isn't feasible. If that's the case, then should we simply abandon any attempt to represent the music in some historical context? Maybe our recipe will take some thoughtful blending of ingredients.

The Historically Informed Performance
The words sure sound good, but what is a historically informed performance? A good definition is the performance of old music on modern instruments that takes into consideration the historical context and performance practices of the period. No one would argue that the modern brass quintet can't brilliantly perform the ensemble music of Renaissance, but we can add another dimension to our performances by intelligently incorporating some of the recognized performance practices of the day.

Start Your Edition—Dynamics, Articulation, and Instrumentation

Music from 1600 comes to us without specified instrumentation, articulation, or dynamics. The omission of these details doesn't mean that that the music was performed without them; it simply means that they weren't notated by the composer and were most often left to the player's discretion. For dynamics, plot out a balanced scheme that adds variety, shape, and continuity to the music, but avoids sudden, uncharacteristic dynamic changes within a phrase. Renaissance wind players didn't slur notes the way we do today. Rather, they articulated using a variety of syllables to group notes together. A combination of slurring and tonguing for smoother, more elegantly articulated passages makes good sense on modern brass. And don't be afraid to vary instrumentation to include higher keyed trumpets for brilliance, flugelhorns for blend, or even to thin the texture by rescoring down to two, three, or four parts. With a little experimentation and common sense, this music can be served up on the menu successfully for even the most discerning chamber music audiences.

Ornamentation—The Icing on the Cake

Maybe the most distinctive performance practice of early music that can spice up our modern edition is ornamentation. In a nutshell, ornamentation is a system of improvisation in which players add their own notes to the music, most often at cadences and in repetitious passages. I know from my own experience that looking at scholarly books on ornamentation has often left me shuddering at the consequence of an inappropriately conceived ornament. But keep in mind that ornamentation is similar to other improvisation; there is a certain musical vocabulary and tradition that has to be explored before one can really feel comfortable. A couple of ways to become familiar with the language are by reading a book like Howard Mayer Brown's *Embellishing 16th-Century Music*, or listening to recordings of early music specialists who have made it their business to master the style. And remember, even though ornamentation implies that notes are added spontaneously, for the purposes of our modern brass performances, don't be afraid to pencil in some ornaments at first. I wouldn't be telling the truth if I said I'd never needed to "work out" some ornaments ahead of time.

Presentation—The Final Touches

Now that you've gotten a few pieces all dressed up with details and maybe even some fancy ornamentation, consider the importance of presentation. Most of the pieces from this period are relatively short by modern concert standards, and a program of thirty 2-minute pieces can sure seem like all appetizers and no main course. Organizing pieces into suites is a way to program early music for an audience more comfortable with 30-minute chamber works than 2-minute songs, and simply requires categorizing the music.

For example, pieces can be grouped by time frame (sixteenth century), type of piece (*canzoni*), location (Venice), or composer (Giovanni Gabrieli). Titles for a suite can be as direct as *Canzoni of Giovanni Gabrieli*, or *The Music of 16th-Century Venice*, or for a real mouthful, a combination of all of the above—*The 16th-Century, Venetian Canzoni of Giovanni Gabrieli*. Also for presentation, don't forget how much our audiences love to be informed, particularly by an expert (or at least someone who seems to know what they are talking about). Writing or speaking about how a suite was compiled or the attention to history that you've brought to an edition, is something that a group should be proud of and want their audience to know about. Revealing some historical trivia—like Elizabethan composer John Cooper "Italianizing" his name to Giovanni Cooperation to increase his popularity—is always fascinating to our listeners. These extra finishing touches, along with the sound judgment we've used in preparing the music, can help us serve up a new, historically informed edition that will be more enjoyable for us to play and more interesting for our audience to listen to. —•

Mouthpiece Whistling and Resistance Mouthpiece Inhalation: Two Unconventional Things to Do with Your Mouthpiece That Enable You to Play with More Open, Freer Sound

Steven Mead

Musically, all of us are "products" of our past musical training, and we instinctively behave and react in a similar way to the way we did when we were very young. So does it mean that our brass performance is predefined for us? Maybe, but my tempting little recipes can enable any brass player to unlearn some bad habits and quickly formulate new ones. A bold promise, yes, but these simple related recipes may balance your acquired knowledge of how to play a brass instrument with the skills (good and bad) that you picked up between the ages of, say, five and twelve.

Here are two techniques to try with mouthpiece alone—really a "starter" to be consumed before the main course, rather than as the main dish itself.

INGREDIENTS:
Your mouthpiece, cleaned inside and out (as per normal!)
A tuning machine or keyboard, or just a very good sense of pitch
A mirror

SERVES:
All brass players who feel the need to play well; in particular, those who suffer from airflow issues and a poorly shaped embouchure.

The first recipe can be served either at the beginning of a practice session or indeed in the middle of one, or mid-rehearsal.

Often our performance can be improved by utilizing more space inside the mouth and at the back of the throat. The benefits of deep breathing are often negated by a restriction in the throat area and at the back of the oral cavity. Tension makes this worse, as does a lack of "vocal awareness." The air simply cannot pass freely through the lips, causing a restriction in tone quality, dynamic range, and pitch range, to name but three. If such a concept is appreciated very early in one's musical life, this area of technique often stays with us a lifetime, but it can be learned, of course.

- Take your mouthpiece and, ensuring the shank has been cleaned, turn it around, then put your lips around the shank, ensuring the lips overlap at least 2 cms (about ¾ inch) from the end of the mouthpiece.
- Hold the mouthpiece with one hand and now breathe in and out slowly. Stay as relaxed and open as possible and use a mirror to check that there is no facial tension.
- Now take the forefinger of the spare hand and jam it into the backbore of the mouthpiece, blocking *just about* all the space. Breathe in again, gently at first, sensing how the body is now trying to take in the air, despite the massive resistance you've created. Relax more and check for facial tension.
- Now increase the velocity of the intake, trying to fill your lungs completely in about 4 seconds, and then exhale for the same duration.
- You are now creating a wonderfully powerful tone chamber inside your mouth and in the throat area.
- Continue this for about a minute (stopping earlier if you become dizzy, faint, or die).
- Reunite mouthpiece with instrument and carry on playing. The benefits of this "dish" are immediate and can be long lasting.

The second recipe uses exactly and same ingredients, but now the mouthpiece is the "correct" way round. I've enjoyed this dish for years and it brings back happy childhood memories of when I was an "angelic" boy soprano! Vocal concepts have always been important to me and this unites a vocal approach with whistling— not whistling with the lips but the natural pitched sounds that emanate from the mouthpiece alone when warm, "round" air is passed through it. Benefits of this are essentially: 1) a more rounded aperture, 2) an awareness of the "bicycle wheel" of control muscles we have round our lips, and 3) control of the moving air from the base of the lungs.

- Hold the mouthpiece as if you are going to buzz on it. Without vibrating, the lips pass a large amount of air through so you're emptying your lungs in, say, 2 seconds for trombone, euphonium, or tuba, maybe 5 seconds for trumpet, and 4 for horn (a real *fortissimo* burst of pure, warm air). Ensure that the sensation in the middle of your aperture is the same as when you had the shank of the mouthpiece in your mouth in Recipe 1.
- Now take a good breath but allow the air to pass more slowly—say, *mezzo forte*—and double the exhalation time. As you do this, imagine the pure sound of your lips whistling (don't worry if you are a nonwhistler) or a pure hummed tone. You might, as you near the end of this breath, hear the first signs of the elusive mouthpiece whistle.
- Now take a similar large breath, but now try to make the exhaled air very warm and very slow. If you hear anything resembling a hiss, there is either a snake in your practice room, or you are forcing/squeezing the air through an aperture that is too "flat."
- Persist with this very soft air and the pure whistle will come. It's possible on a trumpet mouthpiece but very high pitched, quite easy on a horn mouthpiece, and very easy, once you do it right, on anything bigger.
- Use a keyboard or tuning machine to ascertain its pitch, and then try to increase your whistle range to three notes, then up to eight. Don't press too hard on the mouthpiece, and check in the mirror that your eyes are open and you don't look

too weird! Try to sustain your notes for 10 seconds or more. Once you get good, expand your mouthpiece whistling range to include Herbert Clarke's No. 2 finger drills.

This exercise will improve your tone quality as you are forming a rounder aperture and maintaining the "cylindrical" aspects of your air column to where it leaves your lips and as it travels through your instrument. If it doesn't happen right away, don't give up; it may take a few days. Like **Recipe 1,** you could hear an immediate improvement with the "real" playing that follows.

Good luck with this. Enjoy.

Making That Audition Tape—Professional Quality on a Budget

Brad Michel

INGREDIENTS:

2 microphones or 1 stereo microphone
1 twin-mount stereo bar like Atlas TM-1, if using two microphones
1 tall microphone stand like Shure S15A
2 microphone cables
Recording device
A computer with a moderate amount of RAM 500 MB+
Headphones
Time and patience
$500 to $1,000 or friends with $500 to $1,000

SERVES:

Musicians who'd like to record themselves.

As the world of computers and audio recording merge (or collide), it is quite possible that you are walking around with most of a professional digital audio workstation in your backpacks or briefcases. Yes, I'm referring to your computers, any of which can record two channels of CD-quality audio without breaking a sweat. And while there are serious scientific and acoustical forces at work, the recording process is basically musical. You can do it!

The Acoustic and Microphone Placement

Given the choice of recording in a wonderful acoustic with $1,000 worth of equipment or recording in an average room with $100,000 worth of equipment, I would choose less equipment in a good room. Choosing·the space in which you will record is the most important decision you will make. The early reflections in that bathroom you think you sound so good in will only color, not enhance, the sound. Natural results are easiest to achieve in large rooms where reflections offer enhancement without coloration. Churches and concert venues are good choices.

The beginning of the session is the time for experimentation, so plan for one session where you only try various microphone placements. On this night you can adjust to the acoustic, get used to the recording equipment, and document all of your precise settings for a fresh start the next day. Start with the microphone(s) about 8 feet away and 8 feet high. The microphone may need to be higher and closer for tuba than for trumpet. Horn players may want to experiment with a reflecting surface behind the bell. A folding table works well. Generally, as you move the microphone away and up, you are recording more room and less direct sound. As the microphone(s) come down and closer, the sound will be more direct. A good balance will have enough direct sound to engage the listener while having enough room to add a flattering aura. You will most likely be monitoring on headphones and audition committees will most likely be listening on speakers. Recording a balance that is just a little too direct on headphones will produce a balance that should be pleasing on speakers.

Microphone Configurations

Humans are stereo creatures so record in stereo. Stereo will sound more open, even with one musician. If the orchestra requests a mono recording, following the instructions below will make a very mono compatible recording.

If using a stereo microphone, the configuration isn't an issue since the relationship between the two capsules is fixed. If using two separate microphones, they should be mounted on a stereo bar. A configuration that works well for anything from solo instrumentalists to small chamber groups is to have the capsules angled away from each other at 90 to 110 degrees. (*See picture.*) This configuration is commonly referred to as "ORTF."

Level Setting

Setting proper recording levels will be another important chore at your test recording session. Digital recording levels can only go so high. When all of the 16 bits are 1s (no 0s in the digital binary code), that's the top. If you continue to record samples of 16 1s you will be recording a waveform with a flat top. In your trial session, record a signal that is a little too high and you see what these "overs" sound like then lower the levels so that your loudest passages peak at -1 or -2 dB. That's just below the top. Make sure that you don't record the loud passages peaking in the middle of the meters like with an analog recorder. If you record too low, you won't be taking advantage of all of the digital resolution available to you, and perhaps more important is that your recording will sound softer than those recorded with good levels.

The Equipment

Microphones

In a very small nutshell, there are two types of microphone electronics and two main types of pickup patterns. The two types of microphone electronics are dynamic and condenser.

There are very large books written on this subject, so I will make the general comment that condenser microphones are more sensitive so are more suited to classical-style acoustic recording. Sensitive means that the microphones respond more quickly and more accurately to sound in the air. Condenser microphones need a power source. Some are powered by a battery and others by an industry-standard, 48-volt power source referred to as "phantom power." Phantom power is provided by, in this case, the tape recorder, so if you use microphones that need phantom make sure the recorder can provide it. The recorders mentioned below have a phantom power button.

Professional microphones use a three-pin connector called an XLR connector. Sometimes to save space, recorders will have a quarter-inch or eighth-inch tip-ring-sleeve jack for each mic. You will need to confirm this before obtaining cables.

The two pickup patterns you will find are omnidirectional and cardioid (directional). Good results can be achieved with either. Omnidirectional mics have a more natural bass response (ideal for the tuba) and can take advantage of a good acoustic, while cardioids are not as dependent on a good acoustic.

Having two separate mics offers more flexibility, while a stereo microphone can be much easier to use, much like a point-and-shoot camera. With good light and composition, much can be achieved with a point-and-shoot camera!

Most classical recording is done with small-diaphragm microphones rather than large-diaphragm vocal style microphones. Stereo pairs of microphones from companies like Octava, Rode, and MXL offer good sound and value. Rode also makes a stereo microphone called the NT-4. Audio Technica makes a popular stereo microphone called the AT 825.

Recorders

Many exciting products have been introduced in the last few years that make recording, choosing takes, sequencing, and CD burning a relatively easy and efficient process. A single box/software combination can now accept a microphone input and record to software on a computer. One popular product is Digidesign's Mbox. It includes the time-tested Pro Tools software and offers vast online support. Another recent offering is the less expensive USB 122 from Tascam. Tascam includes Cubase software. Both are Mac- and PC-compatible. Another option is a new generation of recorders that record to Compact Flash media. (Yes, like your camera.) You can then transfer these files to your computer via a USB cable or with a Compact Flash card reader. M-Audio makes a recorder called the Microtrack and Marantz also has a feature-packed CF recorder. Note that Apple's GarageBand, included on all new Macs, is a software option for editing and sequencing takes.

The final step is to organize your favorite takes and burn a CD. Most computers come with very basic programs for this purpose. A popular professional program is Toast, from Roxio.

All recorders listed above record CD-quality audio that can be edited and transferred without loss. All recording ideas above can be applied to lower resolution recorders (MiniDisc, cassette, etc.), but transfers from these formats lower the quality of the recording.

Those Digital Words

Sample rate refers to the number of samples (frames, if you prefer) in 1 second. Standard video has 30 frames in a second; CD audio 44,100. Audio wins!

16 bits refers to the length of each sample and is the data that represents amplitude (loudness).

The lowest level recordable is 16 0s (digital black); the highest level 16 1s. There are 65,534 combinations in between.

44.1 kHz sample rate = CD quality

16-bit samples = CD quality

In closing, I recommend that if you decide to record your own audition tape, you allocate plenty of time to learn the equipment and software. These programs are absolutely packed with features, aimed at a variety of users. Learn a little bit each day.

A good recording can be an important element in career enhancement and time spent will not be wasted. If your audition instructions say that the quality of the recording isn't important, ignore it. A good recording is a clear sign that you care, and there certainly is nothing more unmusical than distortion. ➤●

How to Impress a College Faculty Search Committee

Gregory Miller

INGREDIENTS:
General knowledge and/or understanding of university protocol and procedure
Curriculum Vitae
Letters of recommendation
Recital repertoire and master class topics

SERVES:
Anyone seeking a teaching position at a state university or private institution.

The System

It is important to know and understand the system by which a college or university hires their faculty. Most institutions hire faculty as either a tenured-track or nontenured-track position.

Tenured-track positions involve a seven-year process or probationary period before a faculty member is granted tenure. In a nontenure-track position, faculty is hired through an initial contract, renewable according to the terms agreed upon between the institution and the faculty member. In a tenured track position, entrance rank is commensurate to previous rank at another institution or one's performance experience. However, if you have not held a tenured position at another institution, your entrance rank will be assistant professor.

Following a seven-year process in which you must undergo several evaluations, you must petition the university to be considered for tenure generally at the beginning of your sixth year. If successful, tenure will be granted at the end of your sixth year, with rank at associate professor. If not successful, you have your seventh and final year in which to interview for another position. In a nontenured position, a rank of assistant or associate professor may be given, but you are reviewed periodically and your contract is renewable pending the outcomes of the reviews. Although you may find one system preferable to the other, both bring equal advantages and disadvantages.

Curriculum Vitae

In the arena of academia, the presentation of a complete and thorough vitae is paramount. Not to be confused with a résumé, in which just career highlights and dates are noted, the Curriculum Vitae is a much more detailed and comprehensive look into one's career to date. Your Curriculum Vitae (CV) should follow the standard industry format, which should include a short bio, a statement of your teaching philosophy, a detailed listing of recordings, whether as part of a large ensemble, chamber group, or solo recital, published concert reviews, course syllabi, published books or articles, and current projects, if any, currently being pursued. The presentation of an organized, comprehensive, and attractive CV may immediately place you on the short list of candidates.

Letters of Recommendation

Generally, institutions will request letters of recommendation supporting your request to be considered for their position. Although your most positive letters of recommendation may come from close family members, you may want to consider persons who know your work in the professional field. It has been my experience that the best letters come from a combination of those who know your work in academia as well as in performance. In requesting letters from colleagues, be sure to let them know that their letters are being directed to a college search committee and that the most telling letter is one that is detailed but does not exceed a page or page and a half. In addition, the letter should include proper titles and positions of the people to whom it is addressed and should be received within the specified deadlines.

Recital Repertoire and Master Class Topics

Most search committees will review all of the applicants' materials before submitting a short list of potential candidates to their dean or director. If you have been selected as one on the short list, congratulations. That means the search committee was impressed with your CV, recordings, and letters of recommendation. Your day on campus will undoubtedly involve a breakfast with the search committee, a tour of the campus, a meeting with the dean or director of the school, and finally a master class and recital.

In preparing your recital, be sure to choose works that you play well, have performed many times in public, and that accentuate the positives of your playing abilities. Most schools will provide an accompanist. Be sure to forward your music to the committee when requested. Most search committees need no more than 30 minutes of music to assess your abilities.

The second and probably the most crucial part of the interview involves your interaction with the students. This will be revealed in a master-class setting, in which you will have the opportunity to work with members of the studio. Because you will not know these students prior to meeting them for the first time in this master class, decide on three or four major topics that you will undoubtedly be able to address unilaterally with any prospective student. My experience has been to choose articulation, rhythm, musical line, and sound production as key points of interest. It's a sheer bet that one student will have a deficiency in one these areas. Use these general topics and expand on your experience and knowledge of teaching them with the students. Do not feel obligated to include your search committee in your discussions with the students. The search committee is there to observe you and to critique how you relate to students.

Above all, present yourself as who you are and be comfortable. Unlike an orchestral audition, the college interview is a daylong process in which the committee takes many opportunities to evaluate all of your positive attributes. ➤●

Playing in a Big Band Trumpet Section

Bob Montgomery

INGREDIENTS:
A sensitivity to the particulars of section playing

SERVES:
Big band trumpet players.

One of the great musical thrills available to a trumpet player is the opportunity to perform in a big band, where the common goal of the trumpet section is musicality of performance as a section. When the members of a section listen carefully to each other and strive for balance, sound, intonation, time feel, articulation, dynamics, and passion of performance, the resulting music can be absolutely electrifying and can achieve wonderful musical heights.

Achieving such a performance requires a group of musicians who have privately prepared the music to as high a level as possible and then also bring several additional ensemble skills to the section. These ensemble skills include:

Balance: This skill requires listening carefully to each other to ensure that all players in the section can be heard equally. When one player becomes louder or softer than the other members of the section, the concept of balance is lost. During a sectional rehearsal it is beneficial to record the section and listen to the recording as a group. Does one part stand out from the group or is there a part that cannot be heard? Listen to the recording four times and each time focus on a single part.

Sound: It is imperative that each member of the section works towards a full, rich, controlled sound, capable of loud, soft, high, low, bright, and dark sounds. It sometimes helps to have each member of the section take turns playing an identical musical phrase to see if each can achieve a similar sound on that same phrase.

Intonation: This skill means listening to each other to ensure that section members are in tune with each other. A thought on tuning that will assist you is learning to tune quickly and accurately. Many young players attempt to tune by playing a long tone and trying to determine whether they are flat, sharp, or in tune, while they play the long tone. Observe a professional performer tune. They play the tuning note for no more than 3 or 4 seconds and then will either place the horn on their lap (they are in tune) or will adjust the tuning slide of their instrument, check again with a tone lasting 3 or 4 seconds, and repeat this procedure until they determine they are in tune. Younger players usually cannot determine whether they are flat or sharp, only because they have not trained their ears to identify the difference. They may hear that they are not in tune, but they are not sure whether they are flat or sharp.

Here is the procedure to train your ears: Play the tuning note for 3 or 4 seconds. Listen to the sound of your instrument compared to the sound of the player you are tuning to. If you feel you might be out of tune, but are not sure whether flat or sharp, do this: move your tuning slide either in or out and play the tuning note again. You will either sound better or worse. If you sound better you may continue to move the tuning slide in the same direction until you sound in tune. If you sound worse, that simply means you moved the tuning slide in the wrong direction. Move it in the opposite direction and play the tuning note again. Continue this until you hear the pitch matching the person you are tuning to. By playing short (3- or 4-second) tuning notes and then adjusting the tuning slide out or in, you will gradually train your ears to hear the pitch more accurately. Eventually you will recognize pitches as being in or out of tune immediately.

Time feel: The section will never swing unless a common time feel is achieved. This means that each member of the section must demonstrate a strong sense of time while remaining sensitive to the sense of time of the other members of the section. The section will never swing if everyone follows one player, all must participate equally. Practicing with a metronome set on beats 2 and 4 will help achieve this individually and as a section. The metronome clicking on 2 and 4 becomes a click track (much like a click track in a recording studio) and relates to the sound of the drummer's hi-hat on 2 and 4. To create this click track, first determine the tempo at which you would like to play and set the metronome to half of that tempo. The clicks now become 2 and 4 of each measure. Most professional musicians have practiced in this manner at some point in their careers and many continue to do so daily throughout their career.

Articulation: An absolute must for any great section. Listen carefully to each other to ensure that the tongued attack, length of note, and tongued release are identical, as are the placement of the attacks and releases within the time feel. The lead player will determine how each note in a phrase will be played, how the overall phrase will be played, and will ensure that it is always performed the same way. It is up to each section player to listen to the lead player's example and always play in an identical manner. Some school bands fail to rehearse articulation, spending all of their rehearsal time on notes, dynamics, and rhythm. Great bands spend as much time on articulation and accuracy of placing notes and rhythms in the "time feel" as they do on other ingredients of performance. Notice the concept of placing notes and rhythms within the time feel, rather than just playing rhythms.

Dynamics: While it is up to the lead player to determine how loud any phrase will be played, and where crescendos or decrescendos will occur, it is up the fourth player in the section to take charge of these musical events. The fourth player listens to the lead player's direction and then ensures that the appropriate dynamic action occurs. All efforts towards balance and dynamics actually begin with the fourth player and work upwards through the section, not the reverse. The lead player is the leader stylistically and he or she determines how the music is to be played. The fourth player in the section is the person who ensures that this actually happens and to what degree it will happen. If the lead player wants more or less, he or she will discuss this with the fourth player.

Passion of Performance: This is the final ingredient that makes any performance of music special. Without passion, a performance can be a rather boring experience, no matter how correct or free from error. I think of passion as being the expression of your love of the music, an excitement in your playing. Excitement here should not be confused with playing louder, faster, and higher, but rather with playing with exceptional and intense musicianship.

If a performance is performed with excitement and musicianship, and if a love of the music is demonstrated, the resulting performance can be a thrilling, rewarding experience.

And Finally: A section should spend time practicing together outside of regular band rehearsals. Take turns going to each other's homes once a week to rehearse as a section. Talk to each other about the music and how you each feel it should be performed. Listen to recordings together and discuss the musicians and the recorded performances. Go to live performances together. Record the section during your sectionals and listen together, and, play, play, play, and enjoy, enjoy, enjoy! ➤●

Practicing Away from the Horn: Mental Preparation in Music-Making

Jennifer Montone

INGREDIENTS:
An upcoming performance challenge
An open, industrious, and creative mind

SERVES:
Anyone who wants to perform at the height of his or her ability, every time.

Whether we're preparing for an audition or solo recital, playing in a group in which we want to contribute our best, or teaching a master class, it is an extraordinary task to always mentally be in top form. Like athletes, a huge percentage of our success is mental. How well we channel our mental distractions, nervous energy, and performance anxiety helps determine how well we can portray the music we love and infuse it with our own emotions, excitement, and passion.

STEP 1: Ways to prepare in order to beat performance anxiety

Reading Materials
Do some research. Luckily, there is a plethora of literature and other resources about mental peak performance. Go to www.dongreene.com and take the performance tests. Check out the great books: *Soprano on Her Head*, *Zen and the Art of Archery*, *The Inner Game of Tennis*, *Psycho-Cybernetics*, *Peak Performance*, and others. To overcome nerves and distraction, one *must* spend time away from the instrument practicing mental toughness.

Tools and Mental Tricks
Part of my practice routine every day is devoted to concentration exercises. It is possible to learn to still the voices in our heads, recover quickly after mistakes, and beat stage fright and dry mouth. One tool I use is an imaginary locker that I fling distracting thoughts into when they arise. One can imagine talking back to the gremlin that is distracting you with its chatter. When I'm especially scared, I also imagine a one-way shield around me that locks out anyone else's thoughts about me, good or bad, and lets me focus entirely on letting the music out. Colleagues of mine use rings of fire, or a forest of protective trees. For difficult solos, I use Don Greene's "centering" exercise. For lyrical pieces, I imagine the musical line floating out of my forehead, up into the sky.

Before performances, I have a very basic meditation exercise consisting of deep breathing and getting into an alpha state by imagining myself slowly walking down a flight of stairs. I then imagine every aspect of "the big day," up to the act of delivering a fantastic, inspiring performance. The exercise stops there; it is best to focus on the process, not the outcome. What we believe and imagine becomes so. The mental picture you create of yourself and your performances will always inevitably mirror the performances themselves.

Basics and Common Sense

Insisting on maintaining healthy brass playing habits will also improve your mental (not to mention your physical) performance. Require yourself to do some yoga or basic stretching every day before you play, both for the physical benefits and for mental calm and concentration. Vow to do 5 minutes of breathing exercises every morning before you pick up your horn. Web sites like www.breathinggym.com and www.home.columbus.rr.com/juliarose/ (click on the master classes link) are excellent resources. Take the opportunity to work with gurus like Jean Rife (*Yoga for Musicians*), Keith Underwood (excellent wind and brass teacher, NYC), Laurie Frink (Carmine Caruso method, NYC), Jim Thompson (*Buzzing Basics*), Sam Pilafian (breathing coach), and others. Let being a healthy brass player and a grounded human being be the foundation for the vocal, creative musicality we all strive for.

STEP 2: Using musical inspiration to keep your mind focused on the correct things

Training Your Musical Ear

Create in the back of your mind a musical library of favorites to remind yourself of why you work so hard: to share gorgeous music with an audience that may walk away inspired, moved, changed in some way. Learn and cherish all great music, classical or otherwise. Emulate beauty, creativity, rhythmic grooves, nuance, and passion wherever you find it. If I have a solo performance or a big orchestra piece coming up, I will research the composer, listen to his other works, or listen to some of the world's most fantastic performers. For example, Jascha Heifitz and Fritz Wunderlich are perfect inspirations for solo works. Renee Fleming's Strauss CD, especially the *Der Rosenkavalier* excerpts, helps me prepare for *Ein Heldenleben*. The Metropolitan Opera's *Ring Cycle* challenges me to try and embody the sweeping, effortless soaring, combined with mysterious detail work, necessary for Mahler symphonies.

Using this Concept in Audition Preparation

For an audition, two months beforehand, I collect CDs of the pieces on the audition list and make a "master tape" (on an iPod, MiniDisc player, CD, or cassette tape) of all of the excerpts. I record not only the official "excerpt," but the whole movement that it is in, or at least the 100 bars before and after it. I then listen to it *constantly*. Also, every few days, I play along with the recording blaring, to train my body and mind so that every time I play the piece, I feel like I am *in* the group, playing my heart out, having a total blast, hearing all the other parts around me, feeling the collective energy, being a part of intense musical conviction—energy, timing, sound, pitch, musical flair. I suggest trying to imagine: I am the third horn of the Cleveland Orchestra under Szell, or fifth horn in the Berlin Philharmonic. I am Dale Clevenger (or Joe Alessi or Bud Herseth . . .) leading his section, playing with incredible colleagues. I am Dennis Brain playing Mozart, I am Sylvia McNair *singing* Mozart. I am an oboe here, a heavy metal band there . . . then at the performance, be yourself, with the brilliance of others in surround sound underneath you, as an inspiration and guide.

STEP 3: Practice tips to tie it all together

Developing a "Mental Preparation Plan"

Practicing performing makes for great performances. I try to organize my practice sessions to train my body and mind to be a more focused and flamboyant performer. Before every excerpt or solo piece, I have a mental preparation plan that I follow every time I practice or perform that material. It is designed to replace nervous or distracting thoughts with productive ones. This is one sample plan that you can use:

1. While I empty my slides in between excerpts or passages, I let myself react: "Ugh, what was *that?!*," or "Ooh, that was actually okay!" or whatever else comes to mind. The judgment rolls onto the floor with the condensation, and I leave it in the past.

2. Next I use productive replacement thoughts. I sing in my head a predetermined twenty or so bars before the excerpt, or how another instrument played it, or the excerpt itself—hearing the group around me while tapping my toes and swaying my head to the beat. If it's a powerful piece, really letting my body rock. If it's lyrical, really swaying.

3. I then do my centering exercise, sing the same musical preparation again in my head, subdivide two bars before I start, breathe deeply for one bar before. . . then I just let go and trust in my preparation and talent.

4. I try not to worry about missing notes. I just try to breathe, subdivide, sing, and *enjoy!*

Practice your mental preparation for a piece every time you practice the piece itself. The key is to allow replacement thoughts and musical inspiration to free us from the paralyzing antics of our brains while performing. If we can make every concert a collaborative joy, every audition an opportunity to inspire and excite, and every time we pick up our instrument a moment we cherish, than we can truly be the luckiest people on earth. ➤●

The Making of the Professional Musician (A Recipe for Success)

Daniel Perantoni

INGREDIENTS:
A plan
Résumé and demo
Audition preparation
Intelligent practice
Main goal of making music

SERVES:
All performers.

All musicians dream of an exciting career in performance and seldom get into the spotlight. Many spend years getting degrees from universities and conservatories, and expect the world to be waiting for them when they graduate. They have the tendency to think someone will do it for them. However, a dream without a plan remains a dream.

A successful career in performance requires talent, conviction, and perseverance. You must know your strengths and weaknesses and study intelligently in order to reach your performance goals. Sometimes rejection can be so frustrating that it can destroy you as an artist. You have to develop the discipline to practice diligently or there is the risk of losing your performance focus. A successful musician has to be able to cope with the sometimes-grueling schedule of auditions, performances, and tours—often times, living away from home. You must be prepared to give up evenings, weekends, etc. in order to succeed. It is not easy!

The most important thing to do is to develop clear goals and outline them. Once that is established, you can develop a plan to success. The plan can be preparing to win a particular job through an audition. Have your up-to-date professional résumé and demo of your best playing ready to send at any given moment.

Your résumé should be a roadmap of your career. It must be honest, neat, and easy to read. Do not waste the reader's time with unimportant information. Always tell the truth, as one false statement could ruin the validly of your résumé. You may need several different versions of your résumé, each for a different specialty. If you are applying for a college teaching position you would stress your best performances plus your teaching experiences and academic skills.

If you are auditioning for a major symphony or a military service band, or a college teaching position, you may be required to prepare a live recording for the first round of the audition.

You have spent many years of practicing and studying, and know you sound as good as or better than some of the professional with lucrative careers. Now prove it!

Follow the instructions of the audition procedures and make a perfect recording. There are no excuses. Although it is more expensive to hire a professional recording person, the difference can be worth it. The more professional the recording, the better you will sound. Record your audition as many times as it takes to get it perfect. I look as this procedure like one who is preparing to compete for the Olympics. You work out all the details and practice until you can perform the list until it becomes a conditioned response. You are not only preparing a professional recording; you are conditioning yourself to play a confident, quality audition at any given moment. Remember that your competition is doing the same!

Many teaching jobs will require you to send a recording—a demo. Never use a recital tape for a demo! Usually the recording will be of poor quality and likely have mistakes. Program your music to demonstrate a wide variety of your talent. Start with a flashy piece—uptempo—wide range—something technical that will grab the attention of listeners and make them want to hear more. Follow this with something slower that shows your best expressive musicianship. Piano accompaniment tends to get boring. Use a variety of instruments to accompany you, if possible. Choose your repertoire to build in excitement and close with a "barn burner." I suggest that you do not put too much on the recording. Usually 20 to 30 minutes is enough. It is suggested that you record an entire movement without splices or edits. If you hear one mistake from anyone on the recording, do it again! If intonation is questionable, do it again! Do not get ridiculous, however, and try for something that is out of your capabilities. It should be well planned, show a variety of your best performances, and be musically entertaining. *Just get your best on tape!*

Preparation never ends. As you progress, competition becomes keener and you have to stay in top shape. Be flexible and be able to perform in any style of music. The more you know, the more you have to draw on.

Often students are unclear of what to practice and how much time to spend on various areas of their practice. I look at it as a matter of percentages. If you are preparing to perform a technical piece, you should increase the percentages of practicing your technique. However, do not neglect the lyrical playing. So I might do 75 percent technique and 25 percent of lyrical practicing. Then if you are doing more lyrical works, increase the percentages but do not neglect the technical. Do the same with dynamics and range. The majority of your practice should be in the "cash register," which is the range where the majority of music is written for your instrument. However, do not neglect your extreme lows and higher registers. The purpose of practicing is making good performance mechanics habitual. All successful players work daily on fundamentals. You must always practice the materials that made you good in the first place.

Successful performance demands the development of good physical habits that will happen naturally, like the simple task of picking up a pencil. Be concerned with the "doer." One can only play as well as he or she hears. Listen to the master performers on all instruments. My favorites are Bill Evans, Chet Baker, and Frank Sinatra. Imitation is still the best teacher. It is helpful to develop your ear through singing. This will strengthen a closer awareness of pitch, melodic line, and expression. Sing everything in your mind while performing.

Musicality is best achieved when the participant is purposefully sensitive to the feelings being expressed through music. Performers often concentrate so much on the technical manipulations of their instrument that they become insensitive to the expressive feelings of the music. The end product (musicality) is of primary importance for our activities when performing music. The successful musician will be sensitive to the feelings expressed by the music and will be able to transmit these feelings through his or her instrument.

You must combine all the good ingredients learned through practice into becoming one conditioned response. You have to put it all together (air flow, embouchure, tonguing, etc.) into one concentration, which is the making of music! ➤●

Bad Habits Work: A Recipe for Replacing the Old with the New

Marc Reese

INGREDIENTS:
Patience. Good ears. A lot of air. Etude books (to taste).

SERVES:
Efficiency-seeking brass players.

When I first started teaching at the college level, I was shocked by the large number of good-sounding brass players who, upon close examination, had a number of bad habits often attributed to very young players. I was confused as to why these students (and the students I encountered in master classes) had never corrected the bad habits formed during their initial years of study. After much thought on the subject, I realized that the reason these students never felt it necessary to replace them is that *they work*!

When beginning to play a brass instrument, students don't have the strength required to hold their chops in place and start the lips buzzing, nor the strength or concept of airflow to support high notes. Under these circumstances, students use whatever means necessary to play. Almost all young players end up tonguing through their teeth and constricting their air flow. Having no recognizable reason to change these habits, students spend their formative years ingraining them into their playing. When they arrive at college, things seem to be working well but what they are not aware of is that their current approach will not "work" forever. Young players are often unaware that they have these inefficiencies. This is primarily due to the fact that their ears are not well developed.

After a few years of consistent exposure to conservatory students, they begin to hear the difference between their playing and that of their more advanced colleagues. Soon their ears become developed enough to understand that they need to improve their technical efficiency in order to be able to execute the musical clarity that they are beginning to hear both internally and externally. It will always be challenging to convince a student to put down their favorite solo and sit in a room practicing saying "ta" instead of "tha." I try to make my students understand that it is imperative that they take care of these issues when they are young. I can attest firsthand that you do not want to be employed as a musician and have to contend with replacing bad habits while trying to perform at a very high level.

The number-one bad habit, bar none, that I observe in most students is that they stick their tongues through their teeth when articulating. These students unconsciously push their tongue through their lips so that when they pull it away the lips will bang together ensuring that they will start buzzing. Although startling your lips into buzzing does work, it causes a multitude of problems. The most obvious of these is a sloppy attack. In addition, the tongue spreads the lips apart and without realizing it you are forced to use pressure to push them back together. This restricts your lips from buzzing freely, reduces endurance, and adversely affects tone quality.

Brass players must replace their "tha" tonguing with "ta" tonguing. It is vital to their success that they understand that they are literally saying the syllable "ta" when they tongue. Say "ta" or any word that starts with a "t" to confirm the correct placement. Many students cannot tell the difference between these two syllables when playing. The difference can be felt when one holds the front of one's tongue against the back of the top teeth along the gum line. The tongue should be held there continuously through the breath and up until the initial attack. It is important to understand that this is only a way to ensure that the syllable "ta" is being used and not the way one actually tongues when playing. It is also necessary to use a lot more air than one may be accustomed to using. This is essential because, to this point, the tongue has been helping jumpstart the buzz and it will now become exclusively the air's job to do so.

The other issue that I encounter frequently is the ineffective use of air. The most common bad habit caused by this unproductive use of air is tension. Air acts as support for the notes that we play and, in its absence, students are forced to find other means of support. Unfortunately, this usually leads to the use of tension as a support system that will drastically affect sound quality and endurance. Tension will frequently become an issue when attempting to play in the upper register. The presence of tension causes the throat to close. With a reduced air column, the air is forced through at a higher speed, thus helping support the upper register. Before long your brain learns that high notes can be achieved through tension and your bad habit is officially intact.

To replace tension with relaxed airflow, it is crucial to understand that notes must be supported. If they are not supported by the air, the body will have no choice but to utilize tension to squeeze the pitches out. To remove tension from your playing, you must develop your breathing. This can be achieved through the use of breathing exercises that teach you to use your air effectively. Get started by spending some time every day playing easy songs or exercises in the middle and low register. Start utilizing a lot of air and focus on remaining relaxed. Use the syllable "oh" when inhaling and exhale using the syllable "toe." This will force the throat to stay open. As it is most challenging to stay relaxed when we play in the upper register, only play as high as you can while remaining relaxed. After several weeks of acclimating to a relaxed approach, you can begin to extend your range. I suggest moving up a half step every two weeks or so. It is essential that the notes feel like they are completely supported by the air stream before you ascend. Also be careful that pressure doesn't creep into your playing in your pursuit of higher notes.

It is very challenging for anyone to replace bad habits with good ones. Patience is key. It is imperative that, when working on any new habits (e.g., air flow, relaxation, and tonguing), you choose material that is very easy and completely unknown. Our brains are extremely powerful and will reproduce the bad habits we used in the past with known pieces. In addition, our brains are tremendously stubborn. Once a habit is learned, it is extremely challenging to replace it. Remember that most bad habits have been present for a long time and your brain is not going to replace that habit with something you work on for a week. Whether you practice your new habits a few minutes or ten hours each day, it still takes your brain six to eight months of consistent practice to exhibit progress and a year or more before new habits start to become consistent and comfortable. Our brains react well to these new habits when practiced first thing in the morning. Starting with old bad habits just reinforces them in the brain before focusing on the new ones. I encourage my students to spend no more than 30 minutes a day focusing on their new habits. I then suggest that they spend the rest of their day focusing on making music. ➤●

Recipe for Successful Programming

Ronald Romm

INGREDIENTS:
Repertoire. Commitment to the music and musicians. Commitment to audience satisfaction.

SERVES:
All brass performers.

Creating and presenting a successful concert is a major objective for all of us, whether we are professional stage performers, professional music educators, students, or amateurs. We want to be successful in our preparation, and successful in the execution and presentation of the music and of the transitional material (either verbal or nonverbal). The result of careful preparation and a great presentation is that our audience will want to hear/see us again. Here is a formula for creating programming that can yield a successful concert time after time.

The First Half

When we are taught about public speaking, we are often told to start our speeches with an anecdote. In a concert presentation, you'll want to have a powerful opening selection, something that catches the attention of the audience. It is a good idea to choose this opening piece for its beauty and/or its flash. (For Canadian Brass, it became "Just a Closer Walk with Thee," the beautiful, devotional hymn, done in a New Orleans style. The arranger was Don Gillis.) You want the audience to be impressed by the beauty of sound and the ease with which you display your musical abilities.

Then, you'll want to present some good solid repertoire to form the substance of the majority of the first half. For the Canadian Brass, it could typically be some Renaissance music followed by a suite of baroque pieces; for specific ideas on repertoire you can go to www.canadianbrass.com.

If the music you have selected is famous, *be careful to play it really well*, so that the audience recognizes its power in its familiarity. If it is not famous, *be careful to play it really well*, so that the performance can serve to reinforce the audience's observations about your beginning piece(s).

Now, if you have an abundance of time in the concert and already have a happy audience on your side, you can play another piece, perhaps something in contrasting style. Finally, you want a powerful conclusion to the first half of the concert (even if there is no intermission, you may want to create a sectionalized approach). Canadian Brass would usually feature some special arrangements of great interest: perhaps Luther Henderson's writing, or some Beatles music, or something to forecast the feel of the second half of the concert.

The first half of a typical successful two-hour concert runs about 47–52 minutes. Intermission runs from 15 to 20 minutes.

Note: If your concert is only scheduled to run for an hour or so, tailor the selections and duration of the selections accordingly. Be sure to read the rules section at the bottom of this article.

The Second Half

You'll need an opening piece for the second half. This may be additional older repertoire, perhaps something classical, or perhaps it could be some new special piece that either you have composed/arranged or something that one of your friends has written. Choose this repertoire carefully. I'll tell you why shortly.

Follow this piece or set of pieces with some solo repertoire to feature an individual player or two. Your major feature of the concert will come next . . . perhaps it will be a specialty piece (Canadian Brass became famous for its repertoire in general and its specialty pieces in particular. You can find videos of "A Tribute to the Ballet" or Peter Schickele's *Hornsmoke*, for reference on www.canadianbrass.com.), a piece with narration, or dance, poetry, singing, or whatever. Finally you will need a really strong "closer." In addition to these items, you'll need an encore or two.

Second half of a two-hour concert should be about 45–50 minutes.

Some Rules

Rehearse often and well.

Prepare the music carefully; learn it to the point of remembering it really well . . . if not completely, then very nearly completely from memory. If the lights go out on stage during the performance, if you lose a part, or if you forget the printed pages at home or in the trunk of a car, you can still play it. (Yes, these things happen, much more often than one would like to admit . . . this is a subject for another article.) Trust your fellow musicians in rehearsal and on stage; they can make or break your performance. Encourage each other with your suggestions in rehearsal as you learn your repertoire together. Be as nice as possible, but be direct with your suggestions and observations. Remember that you are creating a product for a market that is generally quite discriminating, even if not specifically musically trained.

Prepare the transition material as carefully as you do the actual music. We musicians are not generally trained in the art of looking good on stage, speaking well on stage, telling a good story, or moving from spot "A" to spot "B" smoothly. The audience is always very aware of our every move on stage, so practice these things thoroughly. Do be aware that people in the audience already know that you are going to play "the next piece," so rather than saying, " . . . the next piece we are going to play is . . . ," tell a story about the composer, the preparation, or about the members of the group. Everyone loves a good story. Practice telling your stories.

Prepare your bows, entrances, and exits. Practice these over and over. They must look as good as the music sounds.

Befriend the technical crew. They are really important for the successful presentation of a concert.

Most importantly, *never* bore the audience. Program a *shorter* concert rather than a longer one, and be sure that you are really aware of the audience's response to both the music and the transitional material. Keep things moving. If you lose the audience's attention, it is a huge challenge to get it back. Keep the audience engaged. If you are a brass group, avoid playing so loudly that you create pain for your audience. Play well together, play in tune, play well in rhythm. Remember that if your concert includes introductions and jokes, they are *secondary* to the music (but rehearse them really carefully). The musical product always comes first from the stage, and the audience is the most important participant in the concert. Without them, you have only a rehearsal, a taping, or a broadcast—but no concert.

Mix ingredients with care and commitment. Stir over and over until smooth and seamless. Serve with warmth and honesty. ➛●

Buzzin' for Life

Mike Roylance

My recipe for brass players has to do with many things, but primarily focuses on a daily mouthpiece buzzing routine. This routine works for players of any level, from beginning band students to professional brass performers of all ages.

"The quickest way to a golden tone is through mouthpiece buzzing." I'm not sure which of my many teachers told me this, but early on in my career I took this to heart. I remember starting a mouthpiece buzzing routine while I was a freshman in high school, during my marching band's brass warm-up sessions. The routine has surely evolved over the years, but the principle has remained the same . . . that buzzing on your mouthpiece in some form or fashion is an integral part of being a brass player.

INGREDIENTS:
Mouthpiece
Piano, or chromatic tone generator
Air (which is still free, as far as I know)
10 minutes

SERVES:
Brass players of any age or ability.

I've always thought of the mouthpiece as the actual instrument and the horn itself as simply an amplifier. Master the mouthpiece and the rest is simply adjusting the dials, sliders, and knobs that are unique to your amplifier (instrument). Pat Metheny, one of the world's preeminent jazz guitarists, is as much a virtuoso at what his guitar is plugged into, as he is a virtuoso on the guitar itself. I'm fairly sure that Pat Metheny spent many hours mastering his guitar before he became a wiz at the electronics, digital effects, loops, sequencing, and pedals that create the soundscapes that he has become famous for. After mastering your mouthpiece, learn your electronics, i.e., the buttons, effects, dials, pitch tendencies, dynamic limits, resistance tendencies, and colors of your horn through the different registers.

I do not think that you should buzz all day long, as this would kill your chops, but try out this short, 10-minute routine alongside your fundamental routine and I think you will see some amazing results. Not immediate results, but over time you will notice that your first notes of the day feel exactly like your last notes of the day before. No more bad days no more good days, just consistent, predictable, reliable, and strong chops.

Benefits

- Vibrant, rich tone color
- Strength of embouchure
- Flexibility of embouchure
- Longevity
- Ear development/pitch awareness
- Breath control/management
- Accomplishing in 5 minutes what takes an hour on your horn

This exercise should be the first thing that you do during your practice session, kind of a "stretch out and get the blood flowing" session for your chops. Sit down at a piano or with a tone generator and play a C, or whatever pitch your instrument is keyed in. If you are lucky enough to have a piano, play the C in octaves. The pitch that you are playing should be in the same octave as the second partial of your instrument, i.e., one octave above the fundamental or pedal tone of your instrument. Play the piano strongly or make sure your tone generator has sufficient volume not to be drowned out by your buzzing. Throughout this exercise, you should be using a *glissando* between the notes, still being able to recognize the different pitches, but also being careful not to slot or lock into your pitches. This will enable your chops to vibrate at every frequency.

Play the first five notes: C, D, C, B, C, breathe, start again with the C you left off with, and then play the arpeggio including the seventh: C, E, G, B, C. Breathe, play: C, D, C, B, C, A, G, breathe, repeating the G, buzz: G, E, C. Move down a half step and do the pattern in the new key. Continue down in half steps one full octave so that the beginning note will be your fundamental or pedal tone.

Always buzz with a full, rich, vibrant tone, supported by warm air. This exercise should be performed at a *mezzo forte/forte* dynamic and at a tempo so that each group of notes requires the use of one full breath. Always try to keep your tongue down and keep the embouchure setting that you start with throughout the pattern. Do not breathe in places other than where indicated, as these breath points will help to build an even embouchure setting, which in turn helps to even out your tone color through the different registers of your horn.

When you are finished buzzing down to the fundamental pitch, play the same pattern on your instrument, setting the tone generator to the corresponding key. For added benefit and control, play these at a *piano/pianissimo* dynamic, using only one breath for the ride up and one on the way back down.

Try this everyday for a month and see if, in fact, your first notes of the day become more effortless, consistent, and dependable. Your aural pitch will improve dramatically and your tone quality will richen up as well. It will take away all of the excitement of not knowing what kind of playing day you are about to have. This also works great if you have to travel and cannot take your horn with you. After doing this routine once a day on my honeymoon, it only took me one day of actual time on the horn to feel back in shape.

Mouthpiece buzzing is the key to a full, rich tone. If this exercise is not a good fit for you or your students, at least buzz some sort of melody with a reference pitch *every* day.

Enjoy! ➤

Travel Smoothly To-Go: A Recipe for Smooth Touring

Jon Sass

There may be those of you who have not done very much touring and then some who may have toured for years. For brass players who haven't had much experience with touring, you may benefit greatly from this recipe. Those who do tour may discover new items to add to their list. Touring is not for all of us but for many, playing live music is a great way of life as long as one learns the wisdoms of the trade in respect to traveling and discipline. The following ingredients are all useful for domestic as well as international travel. Whether you tour with a brass quintet, big band, orchestra, brass band, or solo, let this recipe be your tour checklist! Many of these items may seem obvious to have along, but then there are some that may raise an eyebrow. I have toured worldwide extensively for twenty-five years with diverse ensembles of different musical genres.

INGREDIENTS:

For Your Instrument

1 or 2 spare mouthpieces

1 long and short warm-up plan

1 practice mute

2 bottles valve oil

1 slide grease

1 cleaning snake for the slides

1 lip balsam

1 proper flight case

1 shower hose adapter

For the Musicians

Patience and tolerance

Passport or valid ID proving your identity

Credit card

Clear and accurate tour

Copy of the contract

Organizer and business cards

Instrument insurance and travel insurance

Suitcase practical for light traveling

Money belt or neck wallet

ID tags on bags

SERVES:
All brass players.

Most professional brass players will experience at least one or two tours in their lives. Common tour types range from one- or two-nighters lasting over a period of time, weekend stints, or longer stints with theatre productions, which involves staying in different countries/cities for more extended periods. As for newcomers, your first tour will most likely be an unforgettable experience. Try to learn from all types of experiences. One important thing to remember is to stay calm in stressful situations! You can learn a lot from this.

There are sometimes different considerations when using the different modes of transport. When traveling with trains make sure that your instrument is put in a place where tourist or other passengers cannot damage your horn with their heavy bags. When going by bus, don't forget the DVDs and the earplugs.

Extra care is needed when traveling by car or minivan—when loading and unloading, do so as quickly as possible. Always have someone watch the bus or car when unattended. When stopping at rest stations, keep your auto parked within eyeshot. At night always park with the back door or trunk against a wall or hard-to-get-at location. Never leave *anything* in the van when you are not around. Take all valuables indoors at night. Do not underestimate the location for a potential burglary.

When flying, I recommend earplugs for long-distance flights. For the dryness that may occur, drink lots of water and go easy on the alcohol. Some say taking vitamin C helps relieve the dryness and stuffy feeling. Try to be one of the first onboard, because you will have more time to store your instrument and more space options. Below are the ingredients, together with explanations of how they can be applied!

FOR YOUR INSTRUMENT

1 or 2 spare mouthpieces: A spare is strongly recommended. When one is lost and you know the next brass shop is a day's drive away, you won't regret having the spare mouthpiece.

A long and short warm-up: One never knows when a train is delayed or suddenly there is traffic and you have to rush straight to the stage. Having a quick warm-up plan will help the gig go much easier.

Practice mute: Hotel staff as well as their guests would appreciate this spice.

Extra bottle of valve oil and slide grease: Horn maintenance.

A cleaning snake for the slides: Horn maintenance.

Lip balsam: This can be helpful when traveling in cold or dry climates.

A proper flight case: A strong professional case should do the trick. When choosing to buy a flight case, make sure that the case has latches that close below the surface. Latches that sit above the surface damage easily in transport. Also, make sure the outer surface is made of fiberglass, aluminum, or strong wood.

Shower hose adapter: These are a big help for those long tours. This is a tool that fits into the leadpipe and is adapted to connect with a shower hose. It should then be attached to the leadpipe for cleaning out the horn interior.

For the Musicians
Patience and tolerance: Touring can be stressful and sometimes filled with surprises. Staying calm is usually a healthy tactic.

A passport or valid ID proving your citizenship: This is needed when crossing borders or the occasional security checks that happen in some lands.

Credit card: A must for the serious traveler. Many hotels need a credit card for checking in, opening phone lines, mini-bar, and pay-television use.

A clear and accurate tour rider: This is the tour blueprint. Without it, you may miss a train or even a gig.

A copy of the contract: This may come in handy should a dispute arise.

Organizer and business cards: You may run into a contact that may be useful for you. Provide your contact information with a business card, and document the information with your organizer or keep in a card file.

Instrument insurance and travel insurance: Having a damaged horn on the road is bad enough, but having to pay the repair costs alone is not necessary. A good uncomplicated instrument insurance policy is advised. Accidents do occur, so health insurance with international coverage is advised.

Items to use for passing time: This includes books, CDs, portable CD player, MP3 player, and music notes for your next project. Having these goodies may come in handy for long journeys and for free days or for free time.

A suitcase practical for light traveling: It would be wise to travel light. It helps keep away overweight costs and makes movement throughout the tour *much* easier.

A money belt or neck wallet: This makes a pickpocket's job much harder and keeps your earnings safer.

ID tags on bags: Often bags that look similar end up in the wrong places. You won't regret taking time to place this on your bag.

USEFUL TIPS

Drink lots of water: It's healthy and does help in avoiding dry mouth on airplanes and in air-conditioned rooms.

Get plenty of rest before the tour: It would be wise!

Make a mental list of your belongings: Don't leave the hotel or club until you run through your list.

Invest in international/domestic telephone cards: Your family and friends will delight in having a call from far away. These cards are usually found in airports, convenience stores, and tobacco and magazine shops, and are often a very good bargain.

Know airline policies in advance: This is essential for checking in big instruments or for permission to carry instruments onboard. Check weight limitations and other useful information.

Arrive earlier for check-in: It will be easier to deal with unexpected complications when time allows. When using a large flight case, notify the airline a day or so before to help avoid unwanted situations.

Do not carry sharp objects (e.g., scissors or pocket knives) and remove flammable, sharp, and suspicious items from your gig bag: When you fly, carry-on bags are always X-rayed. Such items will surely be taken and you may not ever see the items again.

Use "fragile" or "heavy" stickers for your checked flight case: When checking in, ask for a few of these stickers. If you're lucky, the baggage handler will notice it and, hopefully, will treat your horn with care.

Keep your horn and valuables with you or within eyesight always: When leaving the hotel, this extra effort will always pay off.

Eat healthy: Your body will love this!

Have a great tour and safe journey! ➤

Dynamics: Absolute or Relative?

Ralph Sauer

When we learn to read music, our first teacher usually explains that the letter "*p*" means soft and the letter "*f*" means loud. The other markings, *mf*, *ff*, etc., are then explained in relation to soft and loud. As a basic description of levels of sound, this is quite adequate for the beginning player. However, as we start to play more complex music (and in better ensembles), the inadequacies of these simple descriptions become apparent. If *fortissimo* means extremely loud, does it mean that the passage in question should be played as loudly as possible? If the whole ensemble is marked *fortissimo*, does everyone play as loudly as they can? Do the trombones play as loudly as the flutes? I hope not. Musical chaos is the result of this kind of rigid approach to dynamics.

INGREDIENTS:
None

SERVES:
All brass instrumentalists.

More often than not, dynamics indicate a **quality** of sound rather than a **quantity** of sound. In addition, it is also necessary to know if your part is an important, thematic line or a supporting line. It is possible to play a passage marked *forte* with a soft quality (for example, the 2nd trombone solo in the Mozart *Requiem*) and a similarly marked *forte* passage with an aggressive, louder—in decibels—sound (Wagner's *Ride of the Valkyries*). In fact, you must play this way in a fine ensemble. Playing every *fortissimo* as loud as possible is the reason inexperienced brass players very often "get the hand" from conductors.

One of the most difficult sounds to produce on a brass instrument is a *fortissimo* level of sound with a soft quality (Bruckner, for example). Another difficult dynamic is a *piano* level of sound that projects well to the audience. Many times a solo line will be written with a soft dynamic indication (*p, mp*). If we try to play softly (in decibels), the solo will not project. Many years ago, I remember playing some Copland pieces with the composer conducting, and every time I played some small solo that was marked *piano*, he would ask for more. He was after a soft quality of sound, but with a lot more decibels than *piano* meant to my inexperienced ear.

Once we understand what the dynamic markings truly mean, how do we produce them? In the music of Richard Strauss, Tchaikovsky, Mahler, etc., a *fortissimo* can generally have quite a strong accent on each note. This tends to give a more aggressive quality appropriate for these composers. Raising the bell of the instrument at the proper moment can also greatly increase the volume intensity to the listener. The same *fortissimo* marking in Schubert requires a softer sound so, here, less attack (and fewer decibels) would be appropriate.

Also remember that shorter note lengths sound softer to the listener, while longer notes sound louder. Use this phenomenon to your advantage. If you are trying to achieve a loud (in decibels) sound with a softer quality, try to play as *tenuto* as possible without totally destroying the intent of the passage. To achieve a lighter *fortissimo*, put a little space between the notes and don't sustain the sound quite as much. Remember that *staccato* doesn't always mean "as short as possible." Generally, it means "to detach." Of course, composers interpret this differently. For example in Stravinsky, a *staccato* note is usually played very short. In Brahms, the same note would be quite a bit longer. To project a soft—in decibels—sound, playing with the bell up makes a big difference "out front."

To the question, "Are dynamics absolute or relative?" my answer is that dynamics are always relative. Dynamics must be adjusted for the size of ensemble, the size of the performance space, the particular period or style of music, and, most importantly, how your particular part fits into the musical fabric. ➤●

Articulation, Projection, Respiration: Recipes for Improving Three Essential Skills

Susan Slaughter

Here are three training techniques that have worked well for me and my students.

INGREDIENTS:
Real or imagined target (bull's-eye)
Notebook and pencil
Incentive spirometer or Inspiron (Inspirx®)—one very small ping-pong ball encased in a vertical tube that allows one to inhale and, by turning it upside down, exhale
A stopwatch or clock with a second hand
Your mouthpiece
Your instrument

SERVES:
All trumpet and horn players.

Practice and Improve Attacks

- Place a target (bull's-eye) on a wall directly in front of you.
- Make your notes "hit" the target.
- Do this at all dynamic levels and in all ranges.

Practice and Improve Projection

- In a concert hall, pick a target on a far wall or in the balcony.
- Make your sound "hit" the target (wall, balcony).
- Do this at all dynamic levels and in all ranges.

EXERCISES WITH THE INSPIRON (INSPIRX®)

Exercise 1

- Expel all of your air before inhaling
- Note the resistance setting of the Inspiron
- Place the tube of the Inspiron (minus the mouth attachment) into your mouth.
- Start the stopwatch as you inhale through the tube. Use only as much effort as necessary during your inhalation to maintain the ball at the top of the Inspiron.
- When the ball starts to drop, stop the timer and log your time.
- Repeat three times.

Repeat **exercise 1** six more times using different settings on the Inspiron.

Exercise 2

- Return the Inspiron to the original setting.
- Place a piece of masking tape in the center of the column.
- This time, upon inhalation, maintain the ball in the center of the column where you have placed the masking tape.
- Time and log yourself as before and repeat at all settings.

*For exhalation exercises, turn the Inspiron upside down.

Exercise 3

- Take a deep breath.
- Place the tube of the Inspiron into you mouth.
- Note the resistance setting of the Inspiron.
- Place the tube of the Inspiron into your mouth.
- Start the stopwatch as you exhale through the Inspiron. Use only as much energy as necessary during your exhalation to keep the ball at the top (originally the bottom) of the Inspiron throughout the entire exhalation.
- When the ball starts to drop, stop the timer and log your time.
- Repeat three times.

Repeat **exercise 3** six more times, using different settings on the Inspiron.

Exercise 4

- Return the Inspiron to the original setting.
- This time, upon exhalation, maintain the ball in the center of the column where the piece of tape is located.
- Time and log yourself as before and repeat at all settings.

Exercise 5

- Return the Inspiron to the original setting.
- Inhale and hold the tube ½ to 1 inch in front of your mouth (tube is outside of mouth).
- As you exhale, focus your column of air to enter the tube and cause the ball to rise to the top of the column until you run out of air and the ball drops.
- Time and log yourself as before and repeat at all settings.

Exercise 6

- Now insert your mouthpiece into the tube on the Inspiron.
- Place your lips (if possible) around the outside of the mouthpiece.
- Repeat exercise 5 with lips wrapped around the outside of your mouthpiece rim.
- Experiment with different settings.

Exercise 7

- Now place your lips inside the mouthpiece but do not allow them to vibrate (buzz).
- Repeat exercise 5 with lips inside the mouthpiece.

Exercise 8

- Return the Inspiron to the original setting.
- This time blow air through the mouthpiece and allow lips to vibrate (buzz).
- Try a low, medium, medium high, and your highest pitches, keeping the ball at the top of the Inspiron throughout your entire buzz.
- Time and log yourself as before and repeat at all the settings.

Exercise 9

- Try the slurs/*glissandi* shown below. The first time through, *glissando* from note to note. The second time, slur from note to note. Remember to *keep the ball at the top of the column without letting it drop* between intervals. Movement of air keeps the ball up. If you restrict the air at anytime with your tongue or throat, the ball will drop.

Etc.

- Write your own slur/*glissando* exercises.

Exercise 10

- Now pick up your own instrument and play. Remember to keep that air moving through all the registers—or keep the ball up! ➡●

Brass Player Extraordinaire

Phyllis Stork

As any master chef will tell you, the best guarantee of making great food is to start with the finest ingredients. There is nothing sadder than to see a highly motivated and talented player being frustrated by the wrong equipment for their physical needs. Understanding how to select the proper mouthpiece for your brass player, be they beginner or advanced, will set the table for the unrestricted growth of their talents. This recipe outlines the primary considerations for proper mouthpiece selection. *Allez Cuisine!*

PREP TIME:
10 minutes (just enough time to size up a player's lip type)

COOK TIME:
A lifetime's worth of musical satisfaction . . . now, that's cooking!

INGREDIENTS:
Just a bit of knowledge about how to "fit" a player. Oh yes, a mouthpiece is not just some "fast food" item served up in bulk to the masses, but a critical bit of equipment that must be intelligently designed and manipulated to accommodate the unique physical attributes of a given player. If strict attention is given to selecting the proper ingredients, this recipe yields excellent results.

SERVES:
Trumpet and French horn players and their teachers.

The foremost ingredient in mixing up this dish is the proper selection of the inner diameter. Inner diameter is the term used to express the distance from inner edge to inner edge of the inside rim of a mouthpiece.

This parameter is not to be judged arbitrarily, but must be based on the lip structure of the player. This is especially critical for upper brass players. The smaller mouthpiece makes this initial selection process an essential element in the overall outcome.

Generally, there are three major lip types: thin, average, and fleshy.

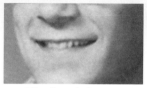 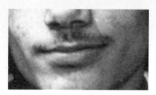 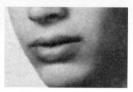

| Thin lipped player | Average lipped player | Fleshy lipped player |

Next, select an inner diameter size that most closely matches your player's lips. More damage has been done early on in the development of young brass players by having everyone start on a 7C than any other single influence. Here's why:

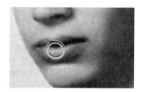

This is what your fleshy-lipped brass player looks like when playing on a 7C. This set up guarantees failure from the outset by setting up the mouthpiece below the *orbicularis oris*. (To see an image of the *orbicularis oris*, visit *Dr. Mouthpiece Archives* at www.storkcustom.com.)

This is the muscle that is responsible for closing down the aperture. (The aperture is the opening in the embouchure through which the air flows.) With the mouthpiece set in this way, the muscle does not have the strength to close down the aperture. Without this ability, the player cannot create the velocity needed to play into the upper register.

Problems can also arise in situations where the inner diameter is too large. Players with thin lips do not have the musculature or ratio of *inherent lip mass-to-surface area exposed* to maintain the necessary aperture setting when using an overly large inner diameter. Players in this situation will experience early fatiguing of the musculature, resulting in problems with endurance, pitch centering, tone production, and range. Yeah, time to reach for the fire extinguisher. This one's going down in flames!

There is a simple formula for getting yourself in the ball park in making this initial selection. It breaks down as shown in the tables on the following page.

Inner Diameter Selection Chart for Trumpet

Lip types	Thin lips			Average lips				Fleshy Lips		
ID in inches	39.5/64	40/64	40.5/64	41/64	41.5/64	42/64	42.5/64	43/64	44/64	45.5/64
ID in millimeters	15.25	15.5	15.75	16mm	16.25	16.5	16.75	17	17.5	18
Stork	SM10		V#7	V(#5)	SM6	V#3		V#2	V#1	V#1.5
Bach	11C	10 1/2C	9C	7C		3C	2 1/.2C	1 1/2C	1C	
Reeves				41		42		43		
Schilke	5a4	6a4	8a4	9	11	13a4	14	16	18	22
Warburton	8	7	6		5	4	3	2	1	
Wick			5		4	3	1			
Yamaha	6	7		11	13	14	16	17	18	

Inner Diameter Selection Chart for French Horn

Lip types	Thin lips	Average lips			Fleshy lips		
ID in inches	40.5/64	41/64	42.5/64	43/64	43.5/64	44.5/64	45.5/64
ID in millimeters	15.75	16	16.75	17	17.5	17.75	18
Stork			M1 – 8	O4, C	O5, CA	O5.5	O6, CB
Schilke		28		30	29, 31	32	
Wick				7	5		4
Alexander	1, 2, 3,		4, 5, MY13	MY9	10, 11		
Giardinelli				C, F, S			
Yamaha	1		27				
Holton			MDC	DC, XDC			

Following these basic guidelines will go a long way in helping many more striving brass players to reach a high degree of skill and satisfaction in their playing.

Special Spices

Beyond selecting the proper inner diameter, there are many other facets of a mouthpiece that control the flow of the air and help to balance the resistance between the player and their equipment. The most significant of these are the cup depth, bore, and back bore. We counsel using these elements with discretion. It has become popular for players to be swept away by abstract concepts of sound while disregarding whether or not their presentation is a healthy balance of technical efficiency and ease of response, coupled with a full bodied tone. A constant and balanced blending of each of these ingredients will result in a truly artistic fare that will satisfy both chef and hungry aficionados of the art.

Bon appetit! ➙●

Spice Up Your Musicality: Dynamic Flavoring for Low Brass Players

Deanna Swoboda

Playing a "background instrument" such as the tuba or euphonium from an early age does not naturally lend itself to a strong development of musicality. While students are developing as young players and musicians, it is important to feed them more challenging, musical literature in addition to their band music. I like to encourage my tuba students to "lead from the bottom" and play as if they have the melody all of the time, with imagination and contour to the line. If a tuba player learns to play the shape of a melody and apply a similar approach to playing the "accompanying figure," the overall sound and musicianship of the band will significantly improve. Here is a new recipe to spice up a young player's musicality.

INGREDIENTS:
Pencil
Metronome
Numbers 1–8
An instrument
A melodic etude
Ear-air-embouchure

SERVES:
The young player who would like to improve their musicality.

As the student begins to prepare a melodic etude or song for a private lesson, they are most likely concerned with learning the notes and playing the correct rhythms. Oftentimes, the etude is played very well, though no consideration has been give to the "song," the contour, or dynamic shaping. We must continually remind our students that we are first singers and then instrumentalists. The instrument is merely an extension of our voices. Speech patterns follow certain shapes and inflections depending upon the question or statement. The importance of emphasis and accent is equally important in music. Take the following five-word sentence. Say it five times in a row, emphasizing a different word each time.

> **My** sister loves ice cream.
> My **sister** loves ice cream.
> My sister **loves** ice cream.
> My sister loves **ice** cream.
> My sister loves ice **cream**.

Each time the sentence is repeated with a different word emphasized, it has a slightly different meaning. It is the same in music. In order to spice up the musicality, it is necessary to emphasize certain notes.

To begin this exercise you will need a melodic etude. Using numbers 1 through 8, 1 equals *ppp* and 8 equals *fff*, you will assign a number to every note in the passage.

1	2	3	4	5	6	7	8
ppp	*pp*	*p*	*mp*	*mf*	*f*	*ff*	*fff*

1. First determine a breathing scheme, based upon composer's markings and following the natural ebb and flow of the phrases. "Pencil in" the desired breath marks.
2. Help the student determine the beginning number (dynamic), ending number (dynamic), and "peak" number (dynamic) of the piece. Numbers will define the dynamic as described above. Pencil in the number beneath each note.
3. Ask the student to place a number on each of the remaining notes in the etude, numbering the entire etude in this manner. Use the natural melodic shape of the piece to determine number values. If the line goes up, the numbers increase. If the line goes down, the numbers decrease.

Next ask the student to *sing* the etude using the assigned number (dynamic) scheme while you play for the student, playing the penciled dynamic scheme. The student will sing using a full resonant voice, with the syllable "O," and follow the dynamics closely. Then have the student play the etude with a metronome using the assigned number scheme. Determine, as in speech, whether the numbering system gives the natural inflections. Freely change the emphasis of the notes to make more sense out of the melodic line, or experiment using opposite numbers. For example, if the note is labeled 1, change it to 8. If it's a 2, then make it a 7, and so on. Have fun changing the numbers (dynamics) and deciding what makes the most musical sense.

Dynamic Pacing
After using the numbers to begin dynamic shaping and musical phrasing, the student will need to accomplish an evenness of dynamic **pacing** within each phrase. Dynamic pacing is defined as moving smoothly from number to number, rather than using terraced dynamics. This can be accomplished by using smooth air, improving the ear, and buzzing the mouthpiece. Combine these ingredients and practice the following exercises to improve the dynamic pacing.

1. Practice a timed breathing exercise away from the instrument, for example **air patterns** on the palm of the hand. Set your metronome to the tempo of the etude. Practice blowing the rhythm of the passage onto the palm of the hand, using a smooth and steady air stream. If the passage is slurred, then simply blow smooth air. Repeat this exercise using the numbered dynamic shape by blowing more air for *forte* notes and less air for *piano* notes with smooth connections. Avoid "bumps" in the air stream. Then return to the instrument and play the passage again, with a smoother sound.
2. To make the passage smoother yet, have the student **half valve** the phrase. Put all of the valves half way down and "buzz" the passage through the instrument. Keep all of the valves halfway down throughout this exercise. Make sure the student is buzzing *forte* the entire passage. This technique requires a strong ear to lead the correct notes

through the instrument. Playing along with the student will enable them to hear the melody while buzzing. After eight measures or so performed this way, ask the student to play the passage normally, once again using smooth air and the dynamic numbering scheme.

A dynamic numbering system is a great way to begin improving a student's musicality. After some thought has been given to the dynamic shape, have them connect the etude with an emotion (e.g., happy, loving, sad, angry) or perhaps write a story or a poem for the piece. Write one word for each note and perform in relation to the words.

There are many recipes for improving musicality. Simply listening to recordings of great musicians is also a fantastic way to increase musical awareness. The musician's job is to connect emotionally with the audience. The end result: *beautiful music!* ➤●

"BURN": To Be On Fire; To Yearn to Do or Acquire Something

David Taylor

INGREDIENTS:
- **BLAZE**–Personal Credo
- **IGNITE**–Study Habits
- **RADIATE**–Necessity for Risk Taking
- **SOAR**–Expansion of Repertoire for Expression

SERVES:
All.

BLAZE

I love playing the bass trombone. Put simply, I love blowing air through the horn in any musical situation. If I have a personal credo, it's:

1) Playing music is a great and blessed way to spend your life.
2) Always be ready to play.
3) Always keep your head in the music.
4) You owe it to yourself to BURN at all times. And,
5) Pass along your information and knowledge.

IGNITE

For many years I've played long tones, broken by articulation, up to six hours a day. After the fourth hour of doing this, you find the bones in your cranium vibrate with the horn. You feel your sound all around you. Your mind and body are focused in this "float," and you "climb into" the sound around you.

This experience of being one with the instrument can be remembered, and through it you learn how to completely balance your articulation, embouchure, and breath support.

I think this must be what warriors describe when they visualize their swordplay in a 360-degree stroke; or what heavyweight champion Mohammad Ali felt when he could perform "the Sweet Science" with equal strength moving backwards and sideways while dancing.

Slow, extensive, meditative practicing has taught me several things:

1) If you want to come up with an individual technique and musical style, keep the horn on your face.
2) You can develop one fundamental technique that enables you to "climb into any sound around you," or put more plainly, enables you to play in any musical genre.

3) Slow, thoughtful practicing enables you to perform with the utmost technical agility and speed.
4) Slow, thoughtful practicing helps you learn to "keep your head in the music."

RADIATE

Read books and go to art museums. Music, literature, and art are totally intertwined. I've found that writers and artists are more articulate about their inner process than musicians, and they write clearly about how they've gotten to their creative heights. It is directly related to what we do. They all write about taking risks. You learn you must take risks; otherwise, "Boring!"

1) Even if you just walk into an art gallery and only notice the diversity of form and style of the work, you still have gained.
   a) Start off with looking at art you immediately relate to. Always remember that, like practicing, if you constantly stay open, you find more to enjoy.
   b) "Stumble" upon an artwork you like.
   c) You will start seeing form, composition, color, and rhythm.
   d) Once you do that, you will begin to understand what the famous sculptor, August Rodin, meant when he said, "There is no such thing as beautiful form, color, or line. There is only one beauty, and that's the beauty of truth revealing itself."

There are lots of ways to interpret that statement. One wonderful interpretation for me is the understanding that perfection in technique is not necessarily the epitome of a great performance. For me, being in the "moment" of the performance translates to perfection.

NOTE: Although it might not happen every day, BURNING in a performance can lead to these "moments."

2) Read what you like.
   a) If you don't like what you're reading, put it down, and move to another book.
   b) Keep trying until you find a book you like.
   c) Once you get into the habit of reading, you might want to return to your earlier "discards."
   d) That "returning" will give you a realization of your self-growth process.
   e) This will help perpetuate the opening of your horizons.
   f) You might realize that there are times when you just have to take the risk of "jumping into the pool, and start swimming."
   g) You might read a statement like I did, by the great writer Henry Miller. He wrote about himself and what it took for him to get to his truth. He realized that if an artist jumped into a pool wearing a life preserver, it would be the life preserver that sinks him. In other words: Risk is vital in the creative process!

SOAR

Through-composed music was my first path into solo playing. I started commissioning music to continue the love I had for the art. I continue to do it, because it's an educational experience. I want to "bring it to the people," while opening my mind and expanding my technique.

I enjoy playing in front of the general public, and when a person in the audience is affected by the music I'm playing, I feel elevated. Audience interaction elevates all involved. I learned that if an audience senses you are genuinely into the music, it could accept any style of music you are presenting.

Personal Note: I wanted to find myself, and find music that directly related to my soul. I found that it is "the search" that is my soul. Hopefully, some of the music I'm bringing into being will last and will be performed by other musicians. Giving something back to the community is a wonderful thing.

Along the path, I've had some luck in premiering a fairly large body of new work for the bass trombone.

Some recommendations to those who want to do this:

1) Approach composers knowing that they are problem solvers. Become a problem solver yourself. Ask yourself, "What do I have to do to get myself out in front of people, playing music that reflects my art?"
2) Even if you don't immediately understand a composer's music or why he is having an impact on audiences, ask him to write you a piece. This is a great way to grow your mind, and if the composer has a track record of impact, a great way to grow your career!
3) If a composer knows you are one who "keeps his head in the music," he will respond directly to it. The virtuoso and the composer are mutually dependent. A composer's reputation is oftentimes dependent on how his music is performed while he's alive! Composers are very aware of this.
4) It is very important to have a definite performance in mind. Composers want concerts, and deadlines are valuable timeframes.
5) Composers grow from being around instrumentalists with freshness and vitality.
   a) Don't be afraid to ask for personalization of the solo part.
   b) Demonstrate your playing for the composer.
   c) If there are problems with the solo part, discuss possible solutions.
   d) More composers will be interested in your playing because of your experimenting.
   e) Oftentimes, their compositions will be reflections of your personality.
6) Be helpful in suggesting accompanying instrumentation. Composers often welcome this. After writing several solo pieces for me, I asked Pulitzer Prize–winning composer Charles Wuorinen to write a trio for bass trombone, tuba, and double bass. Sounds wild . . . he loved the concept. Daniel Schnyder wrote a brass trio for me, for bass trombone, French horn and trumpet. There is a transcription for tenor trombone.
7) If a composer knows you are "championing" his music, you have more financial bargaining power with him.
   a) HINT: Composers earn their living by composing. Help them with money! Work with them to investigate grants, etc.
   b) HINT: Help the composer get media attention. For the composer, media attention is like money in the bank.
   c) HINT: Media attention is money in the bank for the instrumentalist too!
8) Listen to as much varied music as possible.
9) As I wrote earlier, read and go to art museums. Composers love talking to articulate instrumentalists—in between rehearsals!

I've been very lucky to work, study, and be friends with masters. Masters are always studying. They live the art—always burning, and "climbing into the sound around them."

The great composer and arranger Gil Evans and I were walking in Venice one night. He told me that Duke Ellington told him, "If you keep yourself open, you never know who will come along and pull your coat left." ━●

RECIPE

Rhythm Changes for Brass

Kenneth Thompkins

INGREDIENTS:
Horn, melodic etude, metronome, and patience.

SERVES:
All musicians wanting to improve their senses of rhythm.

Performing a piece of music with a great sense of timing and rhythm gives both the performer and listener a feeling of well-being. Brass players can improve their sense of rhythm by examining the meter and then subdividing the beat. Using a metronome is critical in performing this exercise with accuracy. Try to internalize the subdivision when going through the steps below.

Choose a melodic etude that is slow in tempo and is not of extreme technical difficulty. We want to be able to feel the basic beat, subdivisions, two beats to the bar, and one beat to the bar. If this is a long etude, I suggest that you practice only a small section of the etude with this technique. For this exercise, let's say the etude is in 4/4 time and the tempo is quarter note = 80 BPM.

1. The first step is to subdivide the quarter note into sixteenth notes. Set your metronome to 80 BPM and the subdivision setting to sixteenth notes (320 BPM). Play a few lines of the etude with the metronome setting to the sixteenth and repeat.
2. The next step is to subdivide the quarter note into triplets. Set your metronome to 80 BPM and the subdivision setting to triplets (240 BPM). This will probably be a bit of a challenge when playing eighth or sixteenth notes against your metronome. Play a few lines of the etude and repeat.
3. Subdivide the quarter note into eighth notes by setting your metronome to the eighth note setting (160 BPM). Play a few lines of the etude and repeat.
4. Set your metronome to the quarter note (80 BPM), play a few lines of the etude, and repeat.
5. Now let's give the etude a feeling of two beats to the bar by setting your metronome to the half note (40 BPM). Play a few lines of the etude and repeat.
6. The final step is to play the excerpt with the feeling of one beat to the bar.

Examining the various subdivisions of the beat and bar establishes a solid framework in which to develop greater musicianship. While the above exercise has many technical elements, practicing this way will result in greater flow and freedom in your playing.

Quiche à la Musicality

Demondrae Thurman

Teaching someone to be "musical" is one of the hardest and most misunderstood aspects of teaching music. Pianists, string players, and singers tend to have a leg up on brass players with this issue. I could speculate that it is because they start music lessons earlier, but I am not certain of that. Many times brass musicians will use words like "velvet," "chocolate," and "silk" to describe how they would like you to sound or, more specifically, how the music should sound. In some ways, that kind of thinking can be effective. What happens, though, if a person is allergic to chocolate and has violent reactions when ingested? This recipe offers an alternative to using such terms to describe music by substituting them with real musical terms that are defined in any good music dictionary.

INGREDIENTS:
A music dictionary, great recordings (not just brass), good ears, basic understanding of phrase structure, a metronome, a pencil, a good voice (optional), and instrument (substitute for a good voice).

SERVES:
Players who are interested in playing with great expression and style.

If overall musicality is something that you struggle with, listening critically to your favorite recordings can be a great source for information. Keep in mind that you already enjoy these recordings, so you are listening to analyze what it is that you like about the performance. There are four musical elements that you should listen for to determine how they affect the overall performance: form, tempo, dynamics, and articulation.

Form
Invariably, you will discover that the performance highlights the specific phrases and the overall form of the piece/movement. For example, good sentences have a subject and a verb. Several good sentences can make a paragraph. Several good paragraphs make an essay. By now you get the point! The same is true in music. Good phrases in music have certain components (usually an antecedent and consequent subphrase). Several good phrases make a period, or what is more commonly called a section. Of course this cycle continues until you have a finished piece or movement. Again, thinking this way on even the most basic level will serve as the beginning of your new and improved music making.

Tempo

I hear performances that seem to take tempo for granted, which ultimately takes away from the effectiveness of the piece. Typically, composers choose tempo markings for a reason. Do your best to adhere to them. With that being said, I believe the rhythmic content of a piece has a direct effect on the tempo. For example, the dotted eighth/sixteenth rhythm, which I consider majestic or a galloping rhythm, can only be played as fast as it can yet still sound majestic or galloping. If the piece you are working on does not provide a metronome marking or you question the one provided, use your metronome to help establish one that suits the music (not your inadequacies).

Consider places in the music that you could use *rubato*, a *ritardando*, or an *accelerando*. Not all pieces will lend themselves to tempo fluctuations, so please be careful with *rubato*. The ends of some phrases lend themselves well to *ritardandos* while certain times within a phrase an *accelerando* can be used to create a sense of urgency. Carefully measure the use of these concepts, for they are not always applicable.

Lastly, as a brass player, we fight the uphill battle of choosing the correct place to take a breath. Your ability to understand the phrasing and tempo can literally dictate your breath choices. Once those choices have been made, mark them with a pencil. This is not to say that they may not change, but it will give you a great point of departure as it relates to your ability to properly shape a phrase.

Dynamics

Listening carefully to your favorite recordings should disclose a wonderful use of dynamics. Most of the music you play will give dynamic indications such as *mp*, *ff*, crescendos, and the like, but there will be plenty of room for creativity. Do not allow for held notes to maintain the same dynamic level except for very specific cases. Most of the time, held notes lend themselves to one dynamic motion or the other, depending on their location in the phrase. Decide the amount in which you should crescendo or diminuendo so that the change in dynamic is not destructive to the music. Keep in mind that dynamics are relative, so try to expand your range on the loud and soft sides.

Articulation

Brass players tend to be very literal musicians. If there are no markings in a given passage, we tend to play that way. When thinking about articulation, you must consider the type of music you are playing. If the piece is a march of some kind, then syncopations should be highlighted, short note values are usually *staccato*, and long note values usually get their full value. If the piece has a slow tempo with a *legato* marking, think about slurring when possible. This might seem weird but I equate this to the manner in which string players use the bow. String players will play several notes on one bow direction, thus allowing the action of changing notes in the left hand to create the articulation. Brass players do this everyday when practicing lip slurs (which, if done properly, represent some of the most articulate playing that I do). Try to develop a few ways to use your tongue. Using a "T" syllable for defined articulation and a "D" syllable for a slightly less defined articulation is a start.

This recipe has a few assumptions. One is that you have a sound that you like. If you do not find it desirable, then no one else will, either. It also assumes that you are very comfortable with notes and rhythms for they represent the point of departure for any great music making.

Once you are comfortable with the musical choices you have made, sing through them out loud. Try to sing the correct notes, though that is not always imperative. Hearing yourself sing allows you to hear the dimensions of your music making because it takes away the mechanics of the instrument. Ultimately, what you come up with through singing will need to transfer to the instrument. Finally, enjoy your newly found musicality. If done well, people will take notice. ➤●

Mastering Your Ingredients—Or, How to Eliminate Your Measuring Cup

Richard Todd

When speaking to some professional chefs that I know, I am always impressed with their mastery of ingredients. Many hours are spent with even the tiniest of details to create the perfect recipe. They spend years learning about all different aspects of cooking—chemistry, flavor, temperature, using the proper knife or cookware, and everything else involved to perfect their craft. So much time goes into the learning process that they can eventually put together the ingredients without actually measuring them. Their expertise in knowing the proper amount to use eliminates the need for measuring devices.

This does not, of course, infer that chefs do not use such devices; only that they can if they wish. Such care taken with detail, and a good deal of artistic ability, are what set top chefs apart from others in their profession. When I taste a dish and cannot figure out how it was made, I know I am in the presence of a master.

These attributes that take a chef to the top of their game are things that can easily be applied to the world of brass playing. Our ability to pay attention to the tiniest detail in our work should also get us to the point where we can perfect our craft while eliminating our own "measuring cup."

INGREDIENTS:
A goal-oriented mindset
A willingness to be inventive
A willingness to try "wrong," so we better understand "right"

SERVES:
All musicians.

I consider a measuring cup a routine that we do without truly thinking about what we are trying to accomplish. If we are practicing in a way that makes us feel like we are "going through the motions," that is a good example of a measuring cup. That is to say, we know enough of what we do to make something good out of our practice session, but we may not always get to the point where we are confident enough in our work to throw away the cup and try it on our own.

How do we know if we have reached that point in our work? There are probably many answers to that question, so I will stick to a main point or two. In my experience as a teacher,

I have found that young players often lack a confidence in their ability to make decisions for themselves. This can be attributed to a few things—not wishing to anger their teachers, processing *a lot* of information, trying to be "correct" in their approach—the list can go on. Not all young players are this way, but the vast majority of students try their best to make sense of it all, with varying degrees of comprehension. I can relate back to my own years of study—the feeling of needing to "do it right" without really knowing what "right" was. I would work hard, trying to make sure I was doing what my teacher told me to do, knowing that he had a good feel for what I needed to accomplish.

What I didn't know at the time was how much instinct played a part in my development. It seems, as my teacher Vince DeRosa later shared with me, I had a knack for taking his assignments and expanding upon them in my own way. He tells me that I did not always do the work exactly as he prescribed, but made it work for me anyway. I do not think that was planned; I just took his advice and used it as a springboard for my work. I was faithful to his philosophy (and still am), but I was also trying things with as many variations as I could think about to find the best way to perfect the assignment. It just seemed to make sense to me.

I am not suggesting that everyone does things as I have done them, but I believe much can and should be achieved by experimenting with what we already know, and also with what we are currently learning. For example, when we are preparing either for a lesson, a concert, or an audition, how well do we know our material? Could we walk into a lesson and perform our etudes from memory? How about a recital or concerto? More importantly, how about an audition? Our complete knowledge of what we are trying to achieve should be utmost in our minds. I believe that our mastery of the situational ingredients can separate us from others who do not know what we know. It is next to impossible to not feel more confident in our ability when we have mastered our knowledge of the task at hand.

When taking an audition, go beyond working on "the lick" and know in your ear—and mind—not only how it *should* sound, but what *you* want it to sound like. That process is accomplished carefully and methodically in the practice room by training your ear to truly hear what it is you are playing. This practice starts simply enough—listening intently to your sound as you do long tones, focusing on your interval intonation as you do scales and arpeggios, maintaining evenness of your sound throughout your entire range, etc. These are the routines that we too easily do by going through the motions.

Using our base routine as a place of experimentation, we can develop ourselves more thoroughly. If we continue to build upon our desire to better understand our goals, including trying to do things wrongly in order to eliminate choices, we will move more toward our final step—to *eliminate the measuring cup.* Then we can take our place as a master brass player and, even more importantly, a master musician and artist. ➥

Recipe for Jazz Articulation

Adam Unsworth

INGREDIENTS:
Any brass instrument. Jazz performance. Jazz and classical articulation.

SERVES:
Classical brass musicians. Music educators.

"This orchestra couldn't swing if it were hanging from a rope." Have you ever heard or uttered that one after a feeble attempt at a jazz chart during a pops concert? I sure have heard it, and admit to having uttered it on more than one occasion myself. What causes this phenomenon—world class musicians with the finest training and great ears lacking the skill to change styles? It's quite mysterious really. We're not talking about playing an Indian raga here; this is jazz—American-born music—something we've all heard to some extent throughout our lives. My belief is that a good part of this deficiency stems from the classically taught, one-dimensional approach to starting a sound, or, our articulation. It's a problem on all instruments. String players have it rough, too, and are many times the greatest offenders in the previously mentioned pops disaster. Brass guys and gals don't help much either. That "*ta, ta, ta*" tongue doesn't tend to groove too hard.

This is coming from a French horn player? A little background on me, just in case you were wondering. Since the age of ten, the French horn has been my primary instrument. However, from junior high school to the end of my undergraduate years at Northwestern, the electric bass was a very close second. Like many kids, I started out in a rock band, but soon found jazz. From then on I spent a good portion of my musical time and energy laying down the groove as part of the rhythm section of a big band or small jazz combo. This gave me a great start at understanding jazz forms and harmonies, hearing bass lines, and just hanging around people who could swing.

At some point late in my college career I got the itch to try to apply my knowledge and love of jazz to the horn. I went to a local jazz saxophonist for improvisation lessons. The first thing he said after hearing me play was, "Your articulation is all wrong. You have to relearn how to use your tongue. Jazz articulation is backwards." He was right, and "backwards" is a pretty good word to describe the difference in how the tongue is used. I have spent the last fifteen years, off and on, working on getting my jazz feel right on the horn. I think I've finally got it— at least enough to give me the confidence in 2005 to make my first jazz CD, entitled *Excerpt This!*

I don't advocate too much physical analysis of one's playing. Music—the product—should always be where the brain is focused. To tell you the truth, writing this recipe has forced me to think for the first time about how I technically articulate a jazz passage. It's been an interesting exercise, but one that I'm going to do my best to forget the next time I play jazz on the horn. At any rate, here are a few tips that might help take the square out of your chair.

1) *Listen, listen, and listen some more* to great jazz artists. Miles Davis, Stan Getz, Kenny Wheeler, and Robin Eubanks are some of my favorites. There are a lot of amazing players, and they all bring their own personal style, sound, and articulation to their music.

2) Transcribe your favorite tune or improvised solo. If that is too much, just transcribe or work out a favorite lick from that solo. Live with it and play it in different keys to work on your ear. Pay particular attention to varieties of articulation and the different inflections that result. Experiment with ways in which these can be reproduced.

3) *Ta, ta, ta*—It's super clean, there's no doubt about that. It works great at all dynamics too. As classical brass players, we can use just a couple of slight variations on *ta—da, da, da, da* or *la, la, la,* and we've got it. This doesn't work for jazz *at all.* In fact, what really makes a jazzer sound like a jazzer is a huge variety of articulation possibilities that are used freely to express a phrase, very similar to speech. Listen to any Miles Davis recording. Many people say he could "talk" through his instrument. He draws from an enormous palette of articulations and intonations to make his statement. This is what attracts me to his playing, makes him interesting, personal. So how does one physically do this? Obviously it varies with personal style, but a few hints to get started are:

   - Stay away from articulating with the pointed tip of your tongue. In classical music, we point the tongue against our upper teeth to get the *ta* syllable.
   - Instead of articulating forward in your mouth, draw the tongue back a bit towards your throat. This will cause the back of your tongue to curl upwards.
   - With the tongue back, you are in position to do two articulations easily—a "*nya*" syllable with the flattened tip of your tongue brushing forward against the roof of your mouth, and a "*ga*" or "*ka*" syllable with the back of your tongue against your throat. Both are very useful in jazz.
   - Be inventive with your articulation syllables. Constantly mix them up as you create your line. Singing the syllables is often the best way to hear and feel what you are doing. Then, try applying them as you play. The same syllable is rarely used on consecutive notes, as we tend to do in classical music. You hear exceptions, of course—this is jazz! Trumpeter Clifford Brown comes to mind, as he would throw in four or five consecutive *ka*(s) with great effect during a lightning-fast passage. In general, mixing up your articulation is going to be most effective: *do, da, dot, dat, dit, gee, git, ka, kee, nya, whaa.* I could go on. They're all good.
   - Throw in air punctuations and breath articulations frequently. I often feel that I'm barely articulating at all with my tongue, but that the variety of attacks are being produced by air fluctuations. Call them air accents if you like—some rough, some gentle. When doing this, I can really let my tongue have that lazy feel and just roll along with the phrase. Tiny air pops are also what produce "ghost notes"— quick rhythmic inclusions that can greatly help the jazz feel.

4) Let loose, throw all that training aside for a portion of your practice session, and have fun! It is fun and musically invigorating to create. How many of us take time to create as part of our practice? It's okay, too—you won't forget how to play your Haydn or Beethoven while you're working on your Dizzy. In fact, I guarantee it will help your approach to the classical repertoire. I have found it can open a lot of fascinating doors, as well. ➡

Perceptual Pot Luck and Gigs in a Blanket

Warren Vaché

Perceptual Pot Luck: Sight-reading

This was a hand-me-down from Benny Goodman, advice he gave me when I first joined his band.

INGREDIENTS:

10 pounds of music (any kind, any instrument). A chair. A music stand. Your instrument. Your brain.

SERVES:

Teachers, students, conductors, arrangers, mice, men, and the Man in the Moon. Let's face it: who couldn't be a better sight-reader?

Go out and buy 10 pounds of music for any instrument, it doesn't matter. Place your chair in front of the music stand and the 10 pounds of music on the floor to your left. Pick up the first sheet of music and place it on the music stand. Read it, play it. *Do not stop when you make a mistake or go back to correct anything!* The object is to develop your sight-reading, not your ability to know when you've played it wrong. Trust me, everyone knows when you've played it wrong; don't end up practicing to broadcast your mistakes. When you've read the first sheet, place it on the floor to your right. Pick up the second sheet of music and repeat the process. Continue until you have read through the entire 10 pounds of music, then go out and buy 10 pounds more.

Gigs in a Blanket: Improvisation

INGREDIENTS:

As many recordings as you can find. A playback device. Your instrument. Your brain. Your ears. Your passion.

SERVES:

Any and all to varying degrees; that's what makes us all sound different.

Sit in a quiet room and put a recording on the playback device. Listen carefully and do your best to play what you hear. That is to say, pick a favorite solo and play it note for note—inflection for inflection—along with the artist, using only your ears and your brain. Start by listening to players of your own instrument, but don't limit yourself to only that instrument. There is something to learn from soloists on all instruments, and learning to use your ear to hear and understand the solos of these other instruments can provide some startling and wonderful insights. Strive to be aware of what the entire band is doing and to understand as much as you can from a purely playing standpoint.

In this exercise there is no need to transcribe. Transcription is a skill unto itself, and while useful, will improve your skill with a pencil more than your skill with your instrument. Use your instrument as a tool to understand all you possibly can and to express what you've learned. You can analyze solos for harmonic, rhythmic, and melodic content later. The point here is to increase what your ears hear and comprehend, and to make the informational passage from your ears to your fingers as instantaneous as possible. Simply play what you hear. Make your instrument your voice. ➤●

Expanding Your Listening Range and Growing as a Player and Teacher

Tom Varner

In the company of such great brass artists sharing their thoughts in this book, I'm not sure if I have a lot to add, in terms of the purely technical aspects of playing. I would agree with those who stress the importance of a consistent daily warm-up, no matter what the source is, whether it is a "straight" or modified routine from Clarke, Caruso, Farkas, Tuckwell, or Jolley. That daily routine, even if quite short, is an extremely important foundation for a player to "take off" from, no matter what the direction he or she is headed in.

However, as a jazz improviser on the (French) horn, I have learned something else that is crucial to one's growth as a musician: *Keep a healthy balance between consistency and learning something new, and always be open to listening to something that is new for YOU, and for your students.* For me, this is an "essential ingredient" in the recipe for a lifetime of musical growth.

As jazz and classical players, we all know the value of repeated listening, perhaps hundreds of times over, to our favorite Clifford Brown solo, or our favorite Dennis Brain concerto. Knowing every "crook and cranny," every passing sharp 9th tone or every slur or choice of a place to breathe, is an important part of the process of internalizing a common musical language—the process that hopefully gets us on the road to becoming a creative musical individual. But sometimes we and our gifted students get stuck—and I always have to laugh at a talented college senior acting as if he or she knows all the musical answers! This is where "listening range expansion" comes in; we all need a good musical slap in the face once in a while, and some of us more often than others.

Recipe for Listening Expansion and Musical Growth

INGREDIENTS:
Access to a varied music collection. Your college or city library has a surprising variety of CDs sitting there just waiting to be sampled!

SERVES:
All brass teachers and their students.

Here are some examples of nurturing ingredients, thought up today, of opening up some musical worlds for you and your students. Tomorrow, I might come up with another set of examples.

At the end of, say, every second or third lesson, take a few minutes with a student to listen to something that they, and possibly you, have never heard before.

- If you are a classical trumpet teacher (or a jazz teacher, for that matter), listen with your student to Lee Morgan's solo on John Coltrane's "Blue Train," and to Kenny Dorham's playing on his *Quiet Kenny*, and to Don Cherry's playing on his *Complete Communion*. How does it sound "right" or "wrong" to your student? How does the articulation differ? The emotional quality and personal approach of each solo?
- If you are a classical trombone teacher (or a jazz teacher, for that matter), check out the differing styles of Ray Anderson, Robin Eubanks, Steve Swell, George Lewis, Conrad Herwig, Walter Wierbos, David Taylor, or Roswell Rudd. How do they work with the unique qualities of the trombone, and how do they adapt the language of keyed or valved instruments to the trombone?
- If you have rather conservative French horn students, get them to listen to Julius Watkins, Willie Ruff, John Clark, Vincent Chancey, and for that matter, Marie-Luise Neunecker playing Ligeti, and David Jolley playing the George Perle *Woodwind Quintets*.
- If you have a conservative hard-bopper, or a conservative classical trumpet (or any brass) student, open up their "closed-to-other-histories" ears by getting them to listen to the Renaissance cornet of Jean-Pierre Canihac with Hesperion XX, or the baroque slide trumpet of Crispian Steele-Perkins playing Bach cantatas with John Eliot Gardiner. Canihac sounds like a Chet Baker of the 1550s, and Perkins like the Freddie Hubbard of the 1720s! Then, in another lesson, get those students to listen to anything by Dave Douglas, Lester Bowie, Herb Robertson, Roy Hargrove, Cuong Vu, Jack Walrath, or Booker Little.
- If you have young students, make sure they hear Ellington and Louis Armstrong—don't assume that they have!
- And finally, listen, for yourself and with your students, to vocal music—whether from Josquin, Byrd, Schubert, Billie Holiday, Frank Sinatra, or Mahalia Jackson. How can we as brass players learn from the pacing, flow, phrasing, dynamics, and emotional directness of the singer?

When we treat ourselves to listening to something that is *new* for us, it gives us a valuable new perspective. We can sometimes get a sense of what we've been doing right or wrong in recent years, and we can often get a burst of fresh ideas and some new inspiration. And, sharing that "something new" with a student could possibly light a fire and start that young player on a path to a new place that we know nothing about! ➤

The Three Sure Fixes to All Brass Playing Problems ... Also Known As, "The Automotive Approach to Brass Artistry"

William VerMeulen

Fixing the Seemingly Thousands of Problems Pertaining to Brass Players

It seems that every teacher has some "new" solution to the myriad of challenges one can experience as a brass player. Every week I am amazed at the "cure" for this and that, from a new shank or back bore to a special bell that will fix your low range, and from opening your throat to expanding the diaphragm. This incessant groping for the cure gets us farther and farther away from real brass artistry. The answer is simple and available to all. It has stood the test of time and is based on the art form preceding and dictating the craft, and it costs no money. In fact, it is just as simple as driving down the street for a quart of milk and is distilled into three simple automotive analogies, the ingredients below.

INGREDIENTS:
1. Know where you are driving.
2. Put good gas into your car.
3. Keep your engine tuned up.

SERVES:
Anyone wishing to get away from "working" their instrument and get back into "playing" with ease and efficiency.

The Automotive Analogy

The instrument you play is nothing more than your vehicle for musical expression; no different than the car you drive. Let's just say you have a convertible Ferrari sitting in your driveway and you want to travel to a store and get a quart of milk. In spite of the beautiful car you possess, you bring three things to your vehicle.

They are:

1. **Your Own Knowledge of Driving Skills and Your Destination**
   - **Know how to drive a car.**
     If you are only twelve years old and don't have a driver's license, it won't help to have that Ferrari in the driveway. (As a brass player, one must have requisite ability to operate one's chosen instrument.)

- **Know how to get to your destination.**
  You could be a championship racecar driver, but if you don't know how to get to your destination you will get lost and drive around aimlessly. (As a brass player, one must have a clear concept of pitch, tone color and musical plan, i.e., phrasing, style, and interpretation.)

I cannot emphasize enough the importance of having a clearly defined concept of the intended end result. This keeps the player proactive and in the role of "creator" of the product.

2. **Your Own Choice of Gasoline**
   You can have a racing Ferrari parked in your driveway. It may take super high-octane gasoline and if you only put in fifty-five-octane gas, you still will not reach your destination, at least not without tremendous difficulty. (As a brass player, you need to put a lot of good quality air in your instrument. It is a wind instrument, after all.)

There are a couple of ways to check your intake and guarantee that your instrument is properly fueled.

- **The finger breath**
  You can check the quality of your intake by simply putting the index finger of either hand vertically in front of the opening of the lips as you inhale fully. The corresponding sound of the breath with the finger in front of the lips will determine the success or failure of your intake. It should possess a low, ripping sound quality. Any other sound at inhalation is less efficient. (Try taking a full finger breath and then play a note or passage. You will likely notice tonal improvement if your breathing has been a problem.)
- **The law of the tank**
  If you split your air capacity into thirds, you will sound good if you stay in the upper third of the tank. You only have a chance of sounding good in the middle third based on knowledge, experience, and luck. If you dwell in the bottom third of your capacity, you will sound awful.

Excess tension is the bane of the brass player. As you deplete your lungs in exhalation, your body uses tension in ever-increasing amounts to squeeze out the rest of your air. When you stay in the upper third of your capacity, you use the natural elasticity of the lungs to get rid of air. By letting your body naturally deflate you remain more efficient. Having knowledge of where you are in your tank can be very beneficial

Here's an exercise: Let all the air out of your lungs. When you breathe in, split your intake into three equal segments. Become aware of how you feel at each point of the inhalation. You will become more aware when you are in the upper third for optimal efficiency.

3. **Your Own Engine and Transmission**
   In addition to bringing your driving skills and choice of gasoline to your car, you also bring your own engine. Your Ferrari may look beautiful sitting in the driveway but if you open the hood and find a 2-cycle lawn mower engine, or if your Ferrari engine has a bad transmission, you won't get very far. By checking the integrity of your buzz stream you can diagnose inefficiencies and develop a fluid, flexible range.

I recommend using a standard embouchure visualizer to tune up your engine. Play an even glissando from the bottom of the range to the top and check for any gaps or areas of turbulence. The ability to navigate smoothly in all registers is the goal. Listen to the quality and smoothness. An unusually airy buzz is akin to having only five cylinders firing in a six-cylinder engine. You will require more gas (air) to make the engine do the same output. Big gaps in the buzz stream show a transmission problem. As we are aiming for ultimate efficiency, in a sense we are eliminating the old-fashioned transmissions in favor of a continuously variable transmission (buzz stream) that uses the optimally efficient tension level required for the vibrational frequency and dynamic range required. This is extremely beneficial for brass instruments that have long struggled to deal with "breaks" within the normal range of the instrument.

With awareness of these three simple analogies, you can rid yourself of the thousands of problems that seem to creep up in one's playing. Brass playing is ridiculously, magnificently easy! Steer clear of the latest, greatest tool to "fix" what can simply be distilled into one, or a combination of these three brass rules.

Happy driving! ➤●

Pearl Necklace Purée

Charles Vernon

I want to write about one simple subject. *One* note followed by another. Let's call it *a beautiful instant tone followed by another one*.

INGREDIENTS:
Your instrument
A concept of a beautiful tone
Dedication to consistency

SERVES:
All trombonists and bass trombonists.

In every single lesson, clinic, master class, and lecture recital—in every country, city, school, anywhere on this planet that I have been talking and playing the trombones for people—I seem to have one basic topic that I dwell on more than all the rest put together. There are only a handful of trombonists in the world that can do it properly. I have spent my entire playing career having this goal and making it my top priority: *sound*.

Sound is the most important aspect of performing on a musical instrument. It is what listeners hear first and what will stay in their minds. A great musical phrase is made up of one note followed by another until the phrase is completed. The different tensions, whether they are melodic or harmonic, are free for the artist to sing as they wish and tell as a story in song.

What I am doing and teaching is to show how to connect two notes with an absolutely perfect slur and make the *legato* tongue match the natural lip slur, only when a smear will result if it is not tongued.

It is all *one simultaneous event*. The pulse and sound of what you want are dominant in the performing part of the brain. This thought will lead the right arm, lips, tongue, and air to a simple, coordinated process where there is only one perfect way. Remember, the rhythm shows when to move the slide and tongue, simple. The air is moving from one note through to the next note, always flowing. *One beautiful sound emerges out of another beautiful sound . . .*

Good luck! ➤●

Have Something to Say

John Wallace

INGREDIENTS:
Intellect
Heart
Soul
Guts
Bottom

SERVES:
From one person to a potential audience of five billion.

One note. Two notes. A string of notes—a melodic fragment. Head, heart, soul, gut, instinct. After a couple of seconds our minds are made up for us as to whether we are going to enjoy a performance or not. Why?

Communication

If that one note is not merely played, but placed with intent in time, place, and context, continues with an intensity which is apposite to its intention and gripping to the listener, and hands on to the next note in a way which leads the ear, the performer is already on to a winning streak. The listener is hooked into the performer's wavelength and a common bond is set up for two-way communication through the course of the piece or the rest of the recital.

It is not simple.

If you thought it was all about getting yourself note-perfect and working up a performance that satisfied all the current criteria of good taste, manners, and modes of expression, you were only half right—that is only the starting-off point. You have to go further. You have to develop your own distinctive repertoire, your own specialty, or question the consensus view of familiar canonic repertoire. Within this specialty, you have to develop your own individual voice, and then you have to broaden out to embrace the totality of your instrument's repertoire. A tall order. The work of a lifetime. But, infinitely satisfying and rewarding in itself.

Developing

It's difficult to predetermine or self-determine your final career destination in music, but all aspiring musicians must allow themselves a period when they push the boat out to maximize their potential. Jobs that resemble conventional jobs are increasingly scarce in music. To make your way, you have to be prepared to revert to a previous state of society—that of the nomadic hunter-gatherer. You have to chase the work simultaneously to chasing your own optimum standards.

The Musician's Role

Performers have to take on partially the role that bards and minstrels took in former times. Commentators on society. Purveyors of universal truths. Pop and pock musicians are good at giving the impression that they do this. Generally, few classical musicians aspire to the world of ideas at all. They are content to work their instruments to its and their maximum efficiency.

This attitude is not enough any more. "Classical" or "art" music will undoubtedly die unless musicians find something fundamental about the human condition to say through it. The opportunity is there. Many of the pieces that are performed in Western classical music, in effect, struggle with complex philosophical abstractions and go through an extended process of resolving argumentative tensions through a discourse founded in organized sound. (Sonata form is one template for this process.) The level of intellectual engagement is high, and the content and subject matter profound, whether conscious, subconscious, or unconscious.

Nevertheless, in my experience, a disappointingly small proportion of music students at conservatories manifest real interest in music by going to concerts, and few express any real interest in broadening their cultural knowledge base by enquiring about what sort of society produced the extraordinary music that they play. The opportunities are there. The century past—the twentieth—with human achievement and disaster on a colossal scale, was packed with great music that is crying out for advocacy. The twentieth century needs insightful performers as commentators to order and explain what happened in it, to develop an audience for its music so that we can better understand what's happening in the twenty-first.

Practice and Performance

There's never enough time to practice. That is our biggest insecurity as musicians. We all know the frightening Russian regimes of nine hours a day that are guaranteed to turn you into a virtuoso. You do need to get that sort of practice into the mental bank account at some time in your career. Glut practice balances crucially those drought periods when you hit the road. Remember the people, like Frtiz Kreisler, that never seemed to practice, at times like this. They are the ones who go on to the stage fresh. Go for it.

Remember that success and failure coexist side-by-side and feed off each other. You cannot have one without the other. You can not learn without making mistakes. Learn how to convert mistakes into nearer and nearer misses. Take the risks that flirt with success. Safety shots aiming for a nil-nil draw between you and the music lead to an artistic failure. Take risks in practice and then choose the performance option in the heat of the moment according to your level of control on the night.

Perfection

We worry about practice because of the cult of perfection. We use the same mental and physical techniques as Tiger Woods because we all want to be as equivalently perfect in our chosen field. But music is not golf. Perfection has already been achieved hundreds of times over in the CD collections that most music lovers have at home. Live performance should be different. It should take risks. Audiences love thrills and spills. Many of the most memorable performances snatch triumph from the jaws of disaster.

Audiences and Venues

A performance is not an exam. The audience is not a jury. The audience has come for a voyage of rediscovery. Audiences vary and are dependent on the venue they frequent, its locality, its acoustic, its atmosphere, its ambience, its facilities, its tradition of concert-giving. These are background facts we are as well to bone up on through discreet questions when being booked for an event. Enquiries on the day itself are never too late. Once on stage, as perform-ers we quickly suss out audiences and acoustics. Good rehearsal acoustics dry up incredibly and we can, *in extremis*, be left feeling lonely and frightened.

Never rehearse too much in an unfamiliar acoustic on the day (unless you are a brass quintet and it's the only rehearsal you have been able to get together!) It is false security. It's rare that the acoustic does not change substantially. Keep a mental note for your next visit. Dry acoustics are often saved by a close, warm audience and an immediacy of response. Dry sounds horrible to you as a performer, but distance lends enchantment and rarely sounds as bad from the audience. Take all these variables onboard during a concert and vary the performance accordingly, shading, weighting, pacing.

All of the above demonstrates just some of the complex issues that have to be distilled down to that magical first note on stage at the eventual performance. But remember it's that sim-ple: those performers who master the art of having something to say with that one note are the ones who have the enduring careers. ➔●

Developing and Programming Your Inner Coach and Guide

Frøydis Ree Wekre

When riding a bicycle you always look ahead of the front wheel, to avoid hitting stones, holes, or other objects that could throw you off the road. When you play a brass instrument in a concert, rehearsal, or practice room, you also need to train your ability to look (actually, to *think*) ahead—and only ahead.

It is well known that the flow of the air and an efficient embouchure are the two most basic physical conditions for playing a brass instrument. However, many students (and we are all students, in this field) forget that the mind—including the inner ear—is the *number-one tool* for progress and for good results. Many players have experienced, during performing, that a small mistake of some sort can lead to destructive and undesired thoughts. Thus, one starts to think backwards about the music in question rather than forwards. Your own inner critic has crept into your conscious mind, causing problems to your performing.

For the sake of better performing, I suggest that you put this inner critic to work in another function and in another place; let it instead become your own best inner coach and guide! A good coach is usually present at the big sport events, doing pep talks and helping with timing and relevant information whenever possible and appropriate. Musicians are in a way lonelier than most athletes while performing. However, acting in your mind as your own coach and friendly guide ("Follow me, follow me, here is the *great plan!*") could make a significant difference for the sounding result, on any level.

In this recipe I will share some of my thoughts and experiences on this subject.

INGREDIENTS:
Time to formulate an artistic and musical "Plan A" for the music you want to perform. Technical solutions for the execution of this plan. A commitment to consciously be working on developing your self-confidence.

SERVES:
Everybody, from the happy amateurs to the happy (we hope!) professionals—not to forget the serious music students.

Step 1: Acknowledge the strength of the mind and of your thoughts. Try this experiment: Stand with your back close to a wall, close your eyes, relax, and breathe deeply a few times. Then, start to repeat this thought in your mind: "I'm falling backwards, I'm falling backwards," etc. Most people will feel an urge to actually fall backwards after a few times of repeating this thought.

Step 2: Be sure to have a first class plan for the music you will be performing, a great Plan A. This plan must include all the elements of what you really want other people to hear—everything from the *sound* you prefer, through the *intonation*, *rhythm*, *articulations*, and *dynamics*, on to the general *interpretation* and musical *style*, and thus to your *musical storytelling*.

In addition, you need a plan for where to breathe, how much to breathe, and with what speed and confidence to project your air through the instrument at all times in the music. This is the one technical element that most players need to think about during performing, since it usually is the first one to be forgotten in stressful situations.

A good teacher on an artistically high level can help you work out your Plan A. During the preparations, a good audio recorder can also be useful to help determine whether you are satisfied with what you are getting out of this music or not. Another method (and the best one in the long run) is to train your own ability for objective listening to yourself while still working out Plan A. (The last suggestion assumes that you already have a high inner standard, worked out either by your own creativity or by the help of some good teachers in the past. A good slogan to live by: *Set your standards, find your tools.*) Be sure to include good parts of mental practice away from the lips in this stage of programming the Plan A into your mind. Memorizing everything helps a lot also.

Step 3: Be sure that you have performed the music in question more or less exactly according to this Plan A enough times for it to become programmed in your long term "memory bank." Comment: Working out Plan A could be defined as "studying," while repeating the right version(s) enough times for storage in the subconscious part of the mind could be an interesting definition of "practicing."

Step 4: Remember to follow your Plan A during the actual performance—although if necessary, Plan B might also be absolutely okay!

Step 5: Have confidence—in the plan and in yourself and your own ability to carry it out. Comment: This step is a very long term one. Most people understand that physical practice is necessary in order to keep the lips, fingers, etc. in good shape, but the self-confidence is something fragile that one cannot just practice physically into place.

How to develop your own confidence? It might be interesting to know that we tend to get stressed out from three different categories of causes:

a) Generic and environmental heritage.
b) Not being well enough prepared: "Did I really practice enough? Can I play this soft enough? Fast enough? Will I really get most of the notes? The statistic was not all that good during the practice sessions . . . "
c) Sudden, irrational thoughts that pop up in the mind about the size of the hall, about who might be present, and so on.

The self-confidence needs to be built and catered for as much as the breathing technique and the embouchure. This happens during all practice and performing sessions, through slowly building up good statistics and a positive image of one's playing. Dealing with ups and downs in a mature way, and being an encouraging and constructive teacher to oneself is the most important key to this work, in my experience.

Step 6: Have some fun! This is why you started with music in the first place, remember? Give yourself some variation, and use amusing material to work with in your practice times. Be creative and surprise yourself every so often. Nourish your sense of humor, as well. Nobody is going to die if you end up following Plan B instead of Plan A; only your pride might get a small scratch. There are many stories out there of people getting jobs and giving great performances following Plan B . . . so, good luck!

In any case: Make your inner guide get out there in front of the playing and show you the way. ➤●

Euphonium—A Different Brew (What Makes Playing Euphonium Unique?)

David Werden

INGREDIENTS:
Your euphonium
Recordings of euphonium, trumpet, tuba, cello, and voice

SERVES:
Euphonium players and teachers of euphonium.

Euphonium players often study with someone whose major instrument is trumpet, tuba, or trombone. This is not the ideal situation, but it is fine in most cases, and can help the player learn valve technique, breathing, and embouchure. However, euphonium players need to have a special blend of ingredients to produce all the flavors of their chosen instrument. Students fortunate enough to study regularly with an excellent euphoniumist can learn by instruction and example. Students who study with other instrumentalists may need to do a bit more work to develop a well-rounded concept of euphonium playing. Certainly those students can listen to and emulate professional euphonium recordings, but it may be difficult to absorb the complete concept of euphonium based only on recordings.

The Food Pyramid

Just as it is wise to eat a variety of healthy foods, it is wise to listen to a wide variety of music to develop the healthiest euphonium concept. During my euphonium lessons, I have been known to play recordings of violin, cello, trumpet, horn, trombone, euphonium, tuba, and voice. The student must be careful to pick up the appropriate concepts as applicable to euphonium (perhaps with direction from the teacher).

The name "euphonium" is derived from a Greek word that means "pleasant sounding." Therefore, a lovely, dark tone is one key ingredient for a euphonium player. Great euphoniumists are capable of projecting their sound with a relaxed and smooth quality. I have heard players perform a soft melody with band, filling the concert hall to the back row with a smooth sound that didn't seem the least bit forced. A euphonium bell usually points up instead of forward, so it can be more work to get the sound to the audience (without letting an unwanted "edge" creep into the sound).

To develop a large, dark sound, it can be helpful to listen to tuba players. A euphoniumist should not strive to sound like a tuba at all times, but a tuba-like sound is very appropriate in some music, and strength of sound is certainly useful for euphonium. It has been very helpful for me to hear and then play pieces I have heard Roger Bobo or Pat Sheridan play (but there are dozens of other fine tubists and recordings that can serve as inspiration). Hearing a fine tuba artist and trying to emulate the same large sound on the euphonium can result in a dramatic improvement in tone and projection. By developing greater dynamic range, a euphonium soloist will be more able to project a melody line out to the audience while sounding fully at ease.

A lyrical style is necessary for playing some of the wonderful melodies that are given to euphonium in band compositions and solos. A euphoniumist should be able to play melodies with a beautiful sound and a mature sense of melodic line. You can easily hear this in the best euphonium soloists. A recording of Steven Mead playing Saint-Saens' *The Swan* by is an example I like to use to demonstrate smooth euphonium sound and style. Every note of the melodic line is carefully formed and smoothly connected.

A useful way for a euphonium player to learn more about phrasing and musicality is to listen to musicians who are not constrained by the mechanics of a wind instrument. I encourage the practice and programming of vocal and cello literature because either works well on euphonium and because there are so many outstanding recorded performances available.

For vocal examples I try to use folk music or music from the romantic era. These styles are easily accessible for students of most levels of maturity. As a study in phrasing, it is also useful for a euphonium player to phrase according to the lyrics of the song. Singers always strive to bring meaning to the words as they sing, and an instrumentalist should form the melody in much the same way, even when the words are missing.

Cello music is a rich resource and is very appropriate for euphonium (which is called "the cello of the band"). The euphonium student should seek out recordings of fine cellists and listen to the phrasing. String players possess a well-evolved sense of line and phrasing. Learning from them can add maturity to a euphoniumist's playing and will lead to a better euphonium concept. A good example is *The Swan* (mentioned above), which was originally a cello piece but is often played on euphonium.

Along with all the tonal qualities discussed here, important components of euphonium tradition are great facility and impressive technique. Starting about a century ago with Simone Mantia (soloist with the famous Sousa band), euphoniumists have demonstrated technical facility at the same level as the best cornet soloists. Today's players possess full control of multiple tonguing, lip slurs, lip trills, negotiating wide intervals quickly, and more modern techniques such as flutter tonguing and multiphonics.

I often point to trumpet recordings as the highest level of technical proficiency among brass instruments. Generally speaking, the technique one can reach on a trumpet can be achieved on euphonium. By listening to the best trumpet artists, you can hear splendid technical facility and great musical interpretations. Legendary trumpeter Rafael Mendez is my favorite example. Vocalists and violinists strongly influenced Mendez as he was growing up. He wished to have such mastery of his instrument that he could be as expressive as the finest singer and as fluid as the best violinist. Other trumpet players I use as examples include Sergei Nakariakov (especially his flugelhorn artistry) and Maurice Andre, but there are dozens of wonderful players to listen to. One should strive to play the euphonium with the same grace and fluidity as the finest trumpet (or cornet) artists. If you have a chance to hear a recording of Mantia or some of the modern euphonium virtuosi, you will know it is possible.

Simmer Over Low Heat for a Few Years

The skills and musicianship learned by employing these methods will add more ingredients to your musical spice rack. Just as you practice long tones, scales, and arpeggios to develop the technical skills necessary to play difficult music, you should have equally refined skills of sound and style to add the flavor that makes really fine music. Obtain sheet music of a solo for trumpet, tuba, cello, or voice, and then get a recording of the same piece. Work on absorbing the unique qualities of the other solo instruments. Gradually, your euphonium sound will improve to rival the facility of a trumpet or cornet, the musical fluidity of a cello or voice, and the power of a tuba.

As you practice, keep in mind that the euphonium virtually defines "beautiful sound." In every melody you play, take advantage of this and infuse each note of the line with a lovely, flowing sound. Carefully observe the written dynamic range of the pieces you play. Strive for facility in every passage (even slow melodies can benefit from ease of motion). As you do all this you will be developing the foundations of fine euphonium playing. ➡●

Cook Up a Few Noodles (Seventeenth-Century Style): Recipe for Modern Brass Players Playing Early Wind Instruments and Their Repertoire

Jeremy West

INGREDIENTS:
Cornetts, sackbuts, a splash of Gabrieli (Andrea/Giovanni), some choice *pavans* and *galliards*, prime *canzonas*, and perhaps an air or two. Add (optional) chamber organ, when available, to bind the ingredients together.

SPICES:
Historic tunings, ¼ comma meantone being especially tasty. Optional original pitch A = 466. (A = 415 is incorrect for this repertoire, notwithstanding popular belief to the contrary.)

BEST SERVED:
In a fine church or cathedral to a loving clientele of hundreds (or more).

It is often thought that getting involved with early wind or brass instruments as a modern player involves a simple shift from trumpet to cornet, symphonic trombone to narrow-bore baroque instrument, and carrying on as though everything else is equal. Although early instruments do present a new set of technical problems, in actual fact the biggest shift required is in the mind. The technical issues involved when moving from modern instrument to old may appear as a minefield or they may be merely a bed of roses; either way this recipe cannot help you with making the transition from one to the other. But hopefully it will enable you to achieve a fresh approach to sixteenth- and seventeenth-century repertoire.

Method: First set aside your trumpet and your trombone and reserve for use with more familiar recipes.

Taking for granted, however, a reasonable level of technical accomplishment on your early wind instrument, the key ingredient for success in bringing the wonderful and varied repertoire to life is a major shift of the mind. All of a sudden you need to view yourself no longer as a *brass player* but as a *singer*. When playing a musical phrase, you must ask yourself the question, "If I were a singer, would I have sung it as I just played it?" If the answer to this is "no" (as it frequently will be if you are heavily ensconced in romantic and modern repertoire), then you have to go to the questions, "Why not?" "What am I missing here?" and "How can I make that sound more vocal?"

This is a tough bridge to cross for many brass players and one that requires constant self-analysis in the early stages. Do not fall into the trap of blaming the instrument (or the music) if your performance sounds dull. True, not every piece of pre-baroque music is beautiful, and disappointments are indeed to be found here just as they are across the musical spectrum. But generally we can bring new life to an ancient piece by giving it care and consideration, coupled with a vocal and linear style. Try practicing this by playing simple vocal music, taking care to follow the text (even when you do not understand the language).

Once you have embodied the essence of this style of music making (and don't underestimate the difference between this and "regular" brass playing) and can slot into it more or less without thinking, then you have the basis of our stew. Now its time to add the *"noodles."*

"Noodles," or "noodling," to use the corresponding verb, is a popular or slang term amongst early music aficionados for the embellishment of a simple line. And such embellishments in the sixteenth and seventeenth centuries were standard procedure in much the same way as they are today in jazz. The greatest masters (usually the cornetto players, in fact) clearly improvised elaborately and, according to contemporary accounts, with the utmost fluidity and spontaneity. Several of them (Giovanni Bassano, Girolamo della Casa, Francesco Rognoni, to name but a few) published treatises for the benefit of their students, and one of the many exciting things about tackling this repertoire is that we can become their students today by looking at their works and endeavoring to play from them ourselves. If you can, get a transcription of some original seventeenth-century embellishments and practice them until they become a part of your musical vocabulary, not forgetting to thread the phrases together using your new linear and vocal approach to playing.

Finally, in the preparation of your early music performance, take one of the easy pieces of vocal repertoire that you used in the stages above or, perhaps better still, a fine stately pavan, and try out some ideas of your own. At first I recommend you to write out your ornaments in full. So a pavan, for example, which is invariably comprised of a number of repeated sections, is now played straight the first time whilst incorporating your "noodles" in the repeats. The next stage, as you gather confidence, is to use a shorthand (develop a system for yourself) to act as an aide-memoir in performance. And finally, you get to let yourself off the leash, playing freely improvised embellishments on the spur of the moment as the mood takes you.

Your recipe is complete. Yes, it takes longer than boiling an egg, but you are now equipped to breathe new life into old music. Early "brass" repertoire sounded on a well-honed ensemble of cornets and sackbuts can send shudders down the spines both of players and listeners alike. The rewards of mastering these instruments and their repertoire are unparalleled.

If you truly, madly, deeply wish to pass up the opportunity of getting to grips with these wonderful original instruments, but want to borrow some of the music that was written for them anyway using your modern instruments, then try out the above recipe, taking great care to retain the key ingredients of a vocal and linear approach. With a sufficient level of care, a modern brass ensemble can be transformed in its interpretations of early music.

For your listening, look out for recordings by such groups as Les Saqueboutiers de Toulouse, His Majesty's Sagbutts & Cornetts, Concerto Palatino, and Ensemble La Fenice. For your sheet music, seek the catalogues of London Pro Musica and King's Music. ➡●

Peak Performance Stew

Gail M. Williams

Prepare your slow cooker (or choose a date for a recital or have an audition date).

INGREDIENTS:
1 cup "givens" (1/4 c. each: intonation, rhythm, musical intuition, and physical embouchure)
Work ethic
4 cups basic skills (scales, endurance tones, lip slurs, lip trills, unrestricted air)
1 cup mental study
As much as necessary, a top physical condition musician

SERVES:
All brass players.

1. Place your givens in a mixing bowl and stir in work ethic. Place into your slow
   cooker.
2. Next add 1 cup scales, 1 cup endurance tones, ½ cup lip slurs, and ½ cup lip trills.
   Using good etude spoons and recording devices stir for hours. Add into this mix a
   great deal of free, unrestricted air (wish list of 4 liters)—you might use tools, such as
   breath builders, Inspirx®, or any simple visual tools. Kneed this and when flexible,
   add to the slow cooker.
3. Choose and practice a concentration tool such as yoga, meditation, biofeedback,
   and/or Alexander technique. Practice this daily and when you are comfortable, add
   to the slow cooker.
4. Now, find a good aerobic exercise that benefits the musician with endurance, lower
   heart rate, and flexible strength. Strengthen and then add to slow cooker.

Mix all the ingredients together in the slow cooker, stir again, cook for days. Taste (or have
a trial performance for friends) after some time, then place once again in the slow cooker.
Stir and continue cooking 'til ready to be consumed by friends and family (or orchestra committees). ➞●

Getting Off the Page: Three Ingredients for More Musical Playing

R. Douglas Wright

Jazz players learn very early on to get off the page and express their own artistic ideas through improvisation. Classical brass players are generally taught almost the opposite. We are often taught that we must follow every marking on the page at all costs, and that if we can actually accomplish this task, we are then being artistic, well-trained classical musicians. I would argue that the written page is just the beginning, rather than the end result, as we so often think of it. It is our job to bring the markings on the written page to life. There are many ways in which to do this. I offer a brief outline of my way.

INGREDIENTS:
Your instrument
Some music you like to play
Your imagination

SERVES:
Anyone of any age looking to play his or her instrument more musically.

Ingredient 1: Getting On the Page
I separate this first ingredient into two parts. The first part of "getting on the page" involves learning one's instrument to the fullest potential. Essentially . . . *practice!* I spend one to two hours each day working on the fundamentals of playing the trombone with the help of a routine. My routine takes around one-and-one-half hours and touches on every aspect of playing: long tones, lip slurs and flexibility, articulation, loud, soft, high, low, and some exercises that put it all together.

My use for this routine is three-fold. First, I use it to warm up. I'm not too overly concerned with "perfect" first notes as I want to give my chops a chance to limber up before expecting the best out of them. As the chops warm up, the ear becomes more and more critical. Second, because my routine touches on all aspects of playing, I use it for maintaining a certain level of proficiency on my instrument. And third, I use this routine to improve my playing as I strive to do all these mundane exercises and etudes just a bit better today than I did them yesterday. Believe it or not, it can be fun and challenging to try to do so—some days less fun than others. Now that the one- to two-hour warm-up/maintenance/improving routine is done, I'm ready to practice.

The second part of this "getting on the page" deals with the written page, a piece of music. When first learning a piece, especially a solo, try to resist the temptation of listening to a recording first. I believe that prematurely listening to someone else's interpretation of a piece can heavily influence your own playing of the piece. The audience wants to hear what *you* have to say about a piece, not your attempt to sound like someone else playing the piece. I would urge you to try learning the piece from scratch on your own. If you're studying privately with someone, your teacher can certainly help out in this stage. Just hold off on the recordings until you really know the piece and have figured out what *you* want to say with it. Work on the piece slowly. Learn the notes, the rhythms, the technical aspects. Get it under your fingers (or under your slide arm, as the case may be.) As you're doing this work, start asking yourself, "What do I want to say with this music?"

Ingredient 2: Say Something—Anything!
"What do I want to say with this music?" It's a simple question to ask, yet not so simple to answer. One of my favorite questions to ask students is, "What were you thinking about while you played that passage?" Invariably I get responses like, "my sound" or "my technique," or my personal favorite, a shrug of the shoulders and a grumbling, "I dunno." Usually, this is how their playing just sounded: uninspired and uninvolved.

If you don't know what a piece of music is saying to you, start more generally. Is it sad? Is it happy? Is it angry? Try playing passages different ways. Try to make the same passage sound angry, then happy, then silly. The answer may be a combination of all the above, or none of the above. There are no right or wrong answers, simply what speaks to *you*. After you figure out what general kind of mood or emotion you want to portray, start thinking in details that will add support and clarity to your overall statement. If it helps, develop a story that coincides with the music. Then, let this story line dictate your dynamics, your *accelerandos*, your *ritards*, etc. Actually paint your story line with the music. If the main character is getting excited, let the music move ahead a little. If the main character is sad, let it relax and come down dynamically. Write all this stuff in your music. The more mapped out you can be, the better your chances of performing your story in the heat of a performance.

Ingredient 3: Make the Story Your Own—Get Off the Page
Ingredient 3 is the most difficult and the scariest. It's also the most gratifying. Once you've worked out the technical troubles of a piece and then figured out a story line to help your performance take on a more musical shape, it's time to go beyond the page and make the piece truly your own. You can do this by finding something in your own life experience that correlates with your story. If your story line is sad, find something in you that makes you feel that same sadness. If your story line is of joy, find something in you that makes you feel joy. Do the same for anger, for sorrow, for happiness, for any and all emotions. Try to connect to this feeling *before* you've even played a note, before you even go out on stage. Put yourself as much as you can into that mood or emotional state and then come out on stage and share that feeling with your audience.

The audience isn't there to be wowed by your incredible high range or flawless technique. They want to be taken on a journey, away from the office or other everyday stresses of life. If you share with them what you truly feel about a given piece of music, I guarantee they will feel something as well. They will be transported to their own sadness, or rage, or joy. When you have done this, you have given meaning to the composer's notes and lifted them off the page.

This is no longer great brass playing, but meaningful art. Most importantly, striving to do this makes playing so much more gratifying and fun. You might just find yourself playing some pieces differently than those hallowed recordings you used to strive so hard to copy. It has been my experience that people will respond favorably to an honest performance, even if it's different than what they themselves would have done. Sure, you might play things differently than others would. That's *good*!

Remember, the written page is essential. We can't change the composer's notes, rhythms, or markings simply to satisfy our inner muse. However, inside the confines of the written page, we have much more room to express ourselves than most of us use. It seems that many brass players get hung up in the first ingredient of technical proficiency and never allow themselves to go any further. Having said that, no one can hear your musical thoughts if they are buried underneath poor technique and sound. Ingredient 1 is vital. However, remember that technique is a *means to an end*, not the end itself. There needs to be a balance of the technical and the musical sides, or we're only getting half of your picture. I wish you all happy—or sad—practicing. ➤●

With the Right Tool, You Can Do Any Job: Why Playing the Right Instrument Matters

Douglas Yeo

Over the years, I have become increasingly aware of the importance of using the right kind of instrument for diverse kinds of repertoire. Truly, there is no one-size-fits-all instrument, and both dramatic and subtle differences in timbre make choosing the right instrument important. In the postmodern world, where we are seeing the pendulum swing from brass playing as a "concrete" enterprise back to more informed music making, carefully considering exactly what instrument you use before setting out to a rehearsal or concert can greatly enhance both the musical product and your own personal enjoyment.

INGREDIENTS:
An active imagination
Musical curiosity
A passion for reading

SERVES:
Brass players, conductors, audiences, composers, and arrangers, all of whom benefit from this way of thinking.

The brass player who wants to do something more than just show up and play is no longer a rare beast. While for many years brass players sought to conform to a uniform concept (which has led to the lamentable decline of national schools of playing), today players are exercising more interest and curiosity to understand their instrument and how composers intended it to be used.

Modern brass instruments have seen remarkable changes (keep in mind that "change" is not always "improvement") in the last 100 years. Manufacturing techniques have been honed to a high level of quality and quality control, bore sizes have gradually gotten larger, and the myriad choices facing a player who wants to buy a brass instrument are mind-boggling. But while brass instruments have seen remarkable changes, many other instruments in the band and orchestra have not fundamentally changed their sound and playing characteristics. This unilateral change on the part of brasses has led to presentation of many kinds of music being a bit out of whack.

Players should be aware that the most important contribution they can bring to a group is to play contextually. While composers often score dynamics uniformly throughout an ensemble, brasses need to be aware at all times that their directional bells and unique timbre can easily wipe out an entire group. Brass players must always understand what role they play in a given passage. When a conductor gives you "the hand" and says you're playing too loudly, don't think (or, worse, say!), "But I was only playing *fortissimo*." Wrong answer! Play the dynamic that fits the context even if it's different than what's written on the page.

We must also be keenly aware that we can single-handedly damage a colleague's hearing by playing too loudly or by pointing our bells at someone's head. We only reinforce the stereotype of brass players being raw, meat-eating dolts when we use our instrument as a weapon. While it may be a new concept to many, being a sensitive player who is always aware of his surroundings, the acoustic, the amount of space between players, and the appropriate volume level a room can tolerate is what separates fine players from all of the rest.

Historical Context

Because we live in a one-size-fits-all world, where advertising tries to convince us that we need something that everyone else has, brass players often ignore the demands composers make on them. How many times do trumpet players see a part written for cornet and say to themselves, "I'm not going to play *that* thing." When tuba players see a part was originally written for ophicleide, they often think, "There's a reason why that thing went extinct!" (Never mind that most tuba players have never even heard an ophicleide played well.) Trombonists struggle and panic when they see Ravel's *Bolero* on a program, not realizing that the French trombone Ravel was writing for had only a 6-inch bell and a small bore that was similar to today's trumpets.

The first thing an informed brass player needs to do is to develop some historical context. Good players are not formed solely in the practice room. Building a library of excellent books and other resources about instruments, composers, and music history can bring a player back to the world when a particular piece was written. For instance, until the mid-twentieth century, the bass trombone was virtually unknown and unused in France. When we understand that Berlioz and other great nineteenth-century French composers were writing for a section of three tenor trombones, we can appreciate the kind of lean sound they expected to hear from a trombone section. Knowing that Ravel wrote his famous tuba solo *Bydlo* for a small-bore C tuba (a six-valve instrument that is smaller than our modern euphonium) takes the pressure off trying to play it on a monstrous CC contrabass tuba.

Reading books about instruments and their development in various countries helps a player go back in time and bring informed performance practice to the modern ensemble. This is not an appeal for all ensembles to adopt "historically informed performance" like dedicated ensembles of period instruments do. But because the brasses have unilaterally made such dramatic changes in instrument construction in the last century, we can often find we fit much better into a group when we recognize the historical context in which our instrument lives. The big trick is to get outside of our egos: if you use a small bore trombone to play *Bolero*, you are not a coward—you are actually wise.

The Instruments

Trumpets and cornets have very different sounds. In the orchestral world, trumpets for many years did not have valves and their pitches were changed through using crooks of tubing of differing lengths. (This was also true for horns in the prevalve era.) The piston valve cornet opened up a fully chromatic top brass world to composers, but many still liked to exploit the difference in color between the conical-bored cornet and the cylindrical-bored trumpet. When cornet parts are played on trumpet, we take an important voice away from the composer's instrumental palette.

Trombones have a distinctive timbre that can purr or bark. Having a variety of different sized trombones can help us give composers the sound they wanted. Composers often wrote for alto trombone, not because it was smaller and easier to play but because it has a distinctive sound. The same can be said of the contrabass trombone. Contextual playing means that we understand that playing the 3rd trombone part of Berlioz's *Symphonie Fantastique* on a tenor trombone rather than on a large bore bass trombone gives the part a snarl that Berlioz was trying to exploit.

Nowhere is contextual confusion more evident than with the tuba. The evolutionary path that has given us the modern contrabass tuba started with the serpent and then the ophicleide (literally, "keyed serpent"). Both were 8-foot instruments in C. When playing early bass brass parts, we do violence to the balance of the ensemble when we play those parts on 16-foot instruments in CC. For tuba players, the three most important playing concepts are blend, blend, blend.

Conclusion

A little curiosity goes a long way. By trying to understand the composer's intention in writing for a particular brass instrument and learning how those instruments functioned in the ensemble of the time, we can bring a much more interesting and varied approach to our ensemble playing. While curiosity might have killed the cat, I have found that the journey toward more contextual playing has invigorated my musical life in exciting and unexpected ways. ➡●

Notes

Notes

Notes